Reflection of a Soul

Reflection of a Soul

Mary Sturlaugson Eyer

ISBN 0-934126-66-6

First Printing March 1985

Printed in the United States of America

Dedicated to my husband, John, our beautiful and precious daughter, Taniyah Nicole, and my sister, Mary Louise.

If nothing else
Oh, let me learn
To be as my Savior was
Let me gain for myself the quality
In Him that was most
Important to me
If nothing else
Let me learn to love.

*Acknowledgment*

My deepest love and appreciation to Ross and Anita Farnsworth, Max and Ruth Cox, Stephen and Denine Kerr, Mel and Helen Scott, Ruth and Glen Roundy, Lamar and Lula Davis, Van and Gretta Woodward, Delbert and Shirley Rawlings, Linda and Gary Hawkins, Orin and Judy Wood, Joe and JoAnn Cobb, Willis and Saara Werner, Robert and RoseMary Brown, Rex and Ruth Gabbitas, Stanley Wayment family, the Toones, the Fugates, Stella Whitmer, Elmer and Shirley Larsen, the Eyrings, Mary Belle Wortham, Sandra Funk, Luella Tryon, Maxine Thompson, David W. Smith, Chris and Fairy Simms, Marcelynn Kerby, Jack Shafer, Kim Cox, Jeanette Blanchard, Debra Warner, Sherrie Lewis, Isabel Polk, Lynda Bailey, Veda Robinson, Janice Wiseman, Joyce Landreth, Cathy Bryan, Glenna Rose Jorgenson, Mary Beckman, Ora Mae Westover, Kathy Thorsen, Judie Parson, Norma Demmer, Iris DeVaney, Joy Lowrance, Lana Philpott, Lora Williams, Mary Nichols, Vic Mylroie family, Jeri Yamashita, Pres and Anna Parks and so many, many, many others who have given to John and me their unconditional love and support. May the Lord's choicest blessings be yours.

Table of Contents

Preface

23 July 1981

Dear John,

As any concerned mother, perhaps, I've been pondering and praying about what to write you—now as you approach marriage. As I've thought of things, I've jotted them down in note form. Probably some of this will seem fragmented. (When Polonius gave his son, Laertes, advice in *Hamlet,* it sounded as though he were reading from a compiled list a dozen disjointed generalities: "Neither a borrower and/or lender be; To thine ownself be true . . .") It will probably be necessary for you not only to read the words but to ponder them and try to sense what I really mean. Sometimes I feel incapable of articulating well.

I support you in your marriage to Mary. I don't think you two are going into this blindly; I think you've thought of *some* of the problems you're going to face. You'll recognize other problems easily when they occur, though you should try to anticipate them and decide ahead of time how you'll react. For example, there's a good chance that somewhere along the way someone is going to call you—either to your face or behind your back—"nigger-lover." Have you decided how you'll handle that? Will your reaction be different if you're alone than it would be if Mary were with you? Will your reaction be different if it's a member or nonmember? In other words—how tolerant are you going to be, or learn to be, of others' intolerance? Because Mary's an adult and is knowingly placing herself in such circumstances, she'll probably be somewhat tolerant. (Her past experience will be of help also.) But how will it be for both of you when your children are the targets of unkindness and prejudice? I don't think anyone is going to burn a cross on your lawn or throw rotten apples. But there might be parties to which your children are not invited. I think there will be homes from which they'll be excluded simply because of their genetic background. How will you respond?

It seems to me that in all cases your goal must be to do what the Savior would have you do.

Set goals separately *and* together. Then commit to help each other reach those goals—whether they be educational, financial, spiritual or parental. That love is truest which places the partner's interests first. That love is truest which serves self*less*ly—probably a better way to say it. Mary should always come first to you. You are her best possible husband when you help her to be the best wife and mother it is possible for her to be. When you serve her selflessly, then she knows she's the most important person to you. This security allows her, in turn, to be of service to you. You build each other. When the goal of each is to build the other for the kingdom, then a celestial home is created in which spiritual growth flourishes.

You each have a good sense of humor. Don't lose that, but also govern yourselves wisely. There are times when it's fun, casual, and "okay" to be "regular" in front of others. But there are times when total support is needed "in public" and the humor can be saved for "private." Think sensitively of Mary. We must assume that your circle will be the LDS group. This will almost always be predominantly white. You will want to support your dear wife. There will be times you'll be her only anchor of security in a group. Just because you've "adjusted" to the color difference, it will probably be a mistake to assume others have. Always be the safe, secure, stable, constant friend she knows she can count on. In other words, be a blessing to her—not just an entertainer.

Give Mary a blessing. When you are alone for the first time as husband and wife, having prayed and pondered what will be the sensitive and insightful thing to say, place your hands on her head, and—as the patriarch of a newly formed kingdom—bless her with all those blessings you feel she needs at that time. (This includes a blessing on yourself as you bless her "with a husband who. . . .") Do this often. Not only will her needs change, but your ability to be sensitive to her needs will increase as time passes.

Comfort her tears and let her comfort yours. We often love the most and have the most tender feelings toward those whose vulnerability is allowed to show occasionally. We love those who need us.

Be the patriarch in your home. You are the husband, the father. That's what you were born to be; that's what you were trained to be in the premortal existence. Think of your success in a career, *any* career—as secondary. No one cares about your career, really, except that your provide for your family. What's truly important is that you bless your family—that you are tuned in to them and to the Spirit. You are accountable to the Lord. Mary is accountable to you. Your priesthood and your manhood make you literally the head of the home. She is your counselor. When you live in tune with the Spirit, there won't have to be disagreements which would cause you to say, "I'm the head of this family, and we'll do it my way!" A husband and wife who understand their relationship to the Savior and to their Heavenly Father need never argue or become dictatorial.

Be loving and caring and sharing and tender with each other. Be honest in your feelings, your needs, your frustrations, your joys, your sorrows, your hopes, your dreams.

Mary is "famous," a "celebrity" in our little LDS subculture. This probably won't last forever, but for the time that it does, I would imagine you have ambivalent feelings about it. You can't help being proud of her. PROUD! I'm sure you'd like to shout all over town, you're so pleased she's yours. On the other hand, you might—just a little now and then—get tired of it, too. Learn patience in this area. (We can bear anything when we know there's an end in sight.) More importantly, Mary is doing a great work. You must support her totally. If she feels you drag, it will take the zest out of it for her. She truly is an instrument for the Lord. You must support her, even if it seems much of her time is taken up dashing from here to there, speaking, signing books, whatever. Be secure in the knowledge that she's yours. You have her in the warm tender moments of intimacy, when no one interrupts, when no one's attention is diverted. (Mary, you must make sure John never feels second place to your accomplishments. Your most important accomplishment will be to be the best possible wife and mother.)

You two come from *very different* backgrounds. Yet you have a couple of positive things going for you which are the greatest help. One, you love each other. I don't mean to imply the romantic notion that love conquers all. I'm sure it doesn't. What love does do is allow you to be aware and alert and sensitive to each other's feelings, so that you can be tender and caring, putting comforting arms around each other when needed. You'll need to be understanding of each others' position; you'll each need to know where the other one is coming from.

Second, you have the Gospel. Common goals initiated by and through a testimony of the Savior will be your strengths, will eventually wipe out background differences. People who are committed to being obedient, to furthering the work, to serving their fellowman (which includes each other); people who are committed to the truth—THE TRUTH—will have an easier time working out differences. The motives are high, the goals eternal. This will be the most important bond you have.

I love you dearly, John. I'm proud that you're my son. You have the capacity to be all that your wife and your children will need you to be. You will continue to mature, slowly and subtly, and be able to provide the wisdom and calm and love which your family will require. Concentrate on your family, devote yourself to them. There's no greater happiness than the love you'll receive in return.

I support you, and I am here to help you when you need me.

Love,
Mom

P.S. I have more to say about children, but I'll wait until they're on the way.

1
A New Beginning

Though traffic was rather heavy, the car seemed to move smoothly along the road on this late September evening. John and I were on our way to the hospital for the birth of our first child. As contractions spread slowly across my abdomen, I held my breath, closed my eyes and gripped the sides of my seat. The contractions had been growing steadily stronger all day and now the intensity was almost unbearable. John noticed what was happening and reached for my hand. As the contractions peaked, I gripped his fingers tightly for comfort, endurance, and strength.

"Breathe, honey," John ordered me. "Don't hold your breath. Breathe!" He then gave a quick demonstration and motioned for me to join him.

"I don't need to breathe now," I said. "The contractions have begun to subside."

"Well, when the next ones start, breathe like we have been practicing. Okay?"

I nodded my head as I slowly and gently rubbed my hand across my stomach. As I felt the outline of the child inside me, my emotions soared with the realization that the time had actually come for me to give birth to this tiny being that had been growing here for the past nine months (and almost two weeks). At the same time, I felt a bit sad. This baby had become such an integral part of me. Never again would we share time together in the same manner. Thinking about the difficulties I had encountered over the nine-month period—hospitalized twice for dehydration and once for pre-mature labor and suspected loss of the baby—I now smiled. "This is one determined little spirit," I thought to myself. "Sure hope it's not as rebellious!"

I then gave thanks to the Lord as I had so many times during this pregnancy—for blessing me to share in such a special partnership with him. During these past months I had experienced more than ever a special feeling of gratitude for the choice calling of being a woman. Many times since the beginning of the pregnancy I had felt such a warmth of the Savior's love. I had come to know his wisdom and feel his quiet gentleness in great abundance. Many times I had tried to express to him my feelings of gratitude, but mere words just didn't seem adequate for the complete joy I felt. How often tears of inadequacy would flow.

Also, I never failed to give him thanks for the blessing of having his true Gospel in my life. I knew I was richly blessed.

A shiver went through me now as I thought about the many times I had cruelly turned the missionaries away. I felt another shiver as I wondered where I would now be and what my life would be if I didn't have the Gospel.

As I thought of my years in the Church, I could not help but think how blessed this little unborn child was to be born under the covenant. I also thought about these blessed conditions of birth compared to my birth and the birth of my brothers and sisters. This child would be born in a hospital with medical treatment readily available. This child would be born in a nice, warm comfortable room and would not know the threat of freezing to death. He or she would also be wrapped in a nice warm blanket. "What luxuries," I thought as I recalled watching birth for the first time when one of my brothers was born. I could still vividly see the old, faded piece of dress that had been ripped and shaped into a wrapping garment for the baby. Perhaps my memory of the wrapping garment was so vivid because it was one of the only two dresses I had, and I had cried for hours when I saw that Mama had to use it. Even though she tried explaining how impossible it was for her to patch, I had still felt that I could wear it a few more times. As I cried, I watched Daddy repeatedly heating a brick on the one old wooden stove we had. Each time the brick was hot, he wrapped it with an old piece of pantleg, placed it under the old worn quilt to warm Mama's feet. I think Daddy worried often that he would wake some morning to find Mama, the new baby, or one of us, frozen to death. He cared so much. My Mama was so blessed to have had Daddy beside her through each of her nine months of pregnancy. I then realized one blessing my mama had always had. She had never been alone, even though we were so poor. With these memories flashing before me, I again gave thanks to the Lord for my blessings.

Another set of contractions began across my abdomen. This time the intensity of the pain made me cry out.

"Breathe, honey," John said as I doubled over in pain. "Breathe!" he repeated quietly but sternly. "Don't tighten up. Don't fight against them. Breathe, pant, whatever, but don't tighten up."

I tried concentrating on the breathing exercise we had learned and practiced for the past week or so, but couldn't. After several desperate attempts, I tried to think about the meaning of this simple exercise: it was bringing me a step closer to holding this long awaited child in my arms.

"Do you realize a piece of eternity is about to be born to us?" I said to John as I inhaled and exhaled a breath of air between every other word.

John was still trying to get me to breathe, but he became quiet as I spoke. He glanced over at me with a smile and said, "Really is special isn't it, our creation together?"

As the contractions began to ease, I looked at John. "You know something? I'm so happy to be having a baby, but I honestly don't see how Mama endured these pains twenty-two times. And I suppose I haven't even gone through the worst part yet."

"She went through it twenty-four times," John said, seeking to correct me. "Maybe after you go through nine or ten you will know. My guess is she probably became immune to the pain."

"I was correct when I said twenty-two times," I said.

"There were two sets of twins; therefore, she had to go through only one pregnancy for two. *And,* if having nine or ten children is the only way I will know the answer, then I'm destined to never know." I felt a wave of sadness knowing the truth of my last sentence. I really wanted in some way to be like Mama, but one pregnancy had practically killed me. I could not understand why I had had such a difficult time with my pregnancy. After all, I had taken every precaution, from eating right—even eating vegetables and drinking white milk, neither of which I could stand—to getting proper and regular prenatal care, neither of which Mama had ever received.

As I sat comparing my one pregnancy with Mama's many, I reflected over one of the times she was giving birth. As usual, Mama had taken sick during the heart of winter, and the sound of the cold winter wind beating ferociously against the old rag-stuffed windows made the occasion frightening. Generally, we children had to be in bed early, but whenever Mama was having a baby, Daddy didn't enforce that rule. We had all stood huddled around the old stove trying to keep warm and hoping the whole ordeal would soon be over. Miz Sammon was the midwife that always came to deliver Mama's baby. I really didn't like her, and I got the feeling she didn't think much of me either. She always emphasized the "Miz" whenever she introduced herself. She insisted everyone call her "Miz"—everyone except the white folk. My brothers said she wanted black people to call her "Miz" to compensate for the way the white folk treated her. I often heard how she would just laugh like a happy little kid and say "Yas Sur," even when the white folk were telling her how stupid she was. But I knew Miz Sammon was no dummy and was well aware of racism. Despite how much I disliked her, I admired her attitude against blacks calling each other "nigger" and for the way she would reprimand any black she caught doing it. I think she felt as I did. Simply because the whites called us "niggers" did not mean we should stoop to their level, even in jest.

"Git me thet ther kittle of wa'er in hare," Miz Sammon yelled to me from Mama's room. I didn't move. I eyed her coldly, but she did not see me because she had already turned back toward Mama. As I stared at her back, I thought about all the reasons I disliked her. Not only did she look like she had eaten a major portion of the earth's food supply, she was also just a wee bit too bossy for me. She allowed my sisters in the room with Mama but always told me I was too young. "Well, if I'm too young to watch, then I'm too young to work," I thought, deciding for sure that I was not going to take the kettle of boiling water to her.

"Whar is thet wa'er," Miz Sammon yelled as I heard Mama give a painful cry. Miz Sammon was so loud I practically jumped out of my skin. In two steps I had that water in there. I didn't even take time to be concerned about spilling on me.

As I entered the room, Mama was telling Miz Sammon that the baby was coming and to help her up. I stopped short of reaching the old three and one-fourth legged table at the end of Mama's bed and watched as Miz Sammon helped Mama out of bed and over to a big rag that been stuffed with more rags to form a pillow. I watched as Mama squatted over it, still holding on to Miz Sammon for support. Mama was also doing her usual thing, praying!

"Git out of hare." Miz Sammon yelled at me at the top of her voice when she saw me watching. The power and tone of her voice caused me to jump with fright and I dropped the kettle of hot liquid. A big splash of it hit my knee, and I screamed in pain.

"Honey, are you all right?" John asked, sounding worried. I then realized I had just now groaned outloud while remembering how hot that water had been.

Instead of answering him, I pulled up my right pant leg. "See that scar," I said, pointing to it. "I got that when Mama was giving birth to one of my brothers."

After quickly glancing at my knee, John stared ahead as he asked me if the scar was hurting me now.

"No I said, but that's what I was thinking about a few minutes ago."

"Are you all right now?"

Before I could answer him, contractions sent torture through my body, and I groaned with pain. I then began breathing frantically.

"Careful, honey," John said. "Slow down your breathing. You don't want to hyperventilate."

I felt like telling him, "That's easy for you to say." He wasn't in all this pain. Instead, I ignored him and continued breathing hard and fast. His advice proved wise: within seconds I felt myself getting faint with dizziness.

We arrived at the emergency room to find a long line of people waiting for help. Yet when they saw me, none of them hesitated to allow me to move to the front of the line. Hours later I lay in a small private room hooked up to a machine that monitored my contractions and the baby's heartbeat. Drowsiness gradually began to overcome me. Anxious for the baby's arrival I had not been able to sleep the last few nights. I had also been unable to rest in a comfortable position. Each time I had tried resting on either side, the baby would kick furiously in protest. I didn't want to hurt it so I turned to my back, but it was not comfortable for me. I now softly whispered, as I had so many times before, "I love you, little baby," and drifted off into a slumber.

"Honey, are you hurting?" John asked, waking me. I looked at him, and with my eyes wide open said, "Don't touch that cookie batter. Where's the football? Oh no, it's snowing and the flowers will get wet. Did you remember to bring in the rats?" John sat staring at me in shock. Finally I laughed.

"Are you delirious?" John asked, still looking shocked.

"No, but I'm hungry. Plus I want to make sure you don't get bored."

"I am not bored, and I don't think you can have any food, but I'll go ask the nurse."

John had barely left when another set of contractions started. Missing the calmness of his hand, I prayed to the Lord for comfort. Then I thought again of Mama and how I had always heard her praying. I recalled her once when she was looking for a needle to patch some pants for my brothers. (I'm not sure which she spent more time doing, patching clothes or stuffing our shoes with cardboard to cover the holes in the sole.) When she found the needle, she had said, "Thank you, Lord." Hearing her, I proceeded to mock her. "Thank you, Lord," I jeered. "Mama, don't you think you do *anything* on your own? Just once I would love to hear you give yourself credit for something. It's *you* doing it, Mama, *not the Lord.*" I then mocked her again. She scolded me, but I didn't care. I had spoken my feelings, and as I went outside I hoped she would remember what I had said the next time she did something. My eyes now became moist with tears as I thought about how cruel I had been to her. I ached to have her near, to be able to hold her dry, frail hand in mine and feel her love. I closed my eyes tight in an effort to feel Mama's closeness; instead, the baby chose that moment to kick my ribs one last time. I didn't have a chance to think about the pains from the baby's kick as pains from another set of contractions overwhelmed me. Forgetting John was not there, I reached for his hand. But when I cried out, it was Mama I called for. At that moment I felt so alone. But it was not a new feeling. No one could know how alone I had felt for so many years.

I thought about parts of a letter a very dear friend and brother, Dr. Elmer Larsen of Oroville, California, had written to me. "We *love* you, Mary, and know the Lord loves you and is certainly mindful of your needs even though you may sometimes feel like Joseph in Liberty Jail when he had endured so long with 'no sunshine' and all others seemed to have forsaken him. Hang on. Hang in there, Mary. Whatever comes, the Lord has not, nor will not, ignore the service of love you have done for him. It will be for you as with Joseph, if you endure it well. Your experiences will further refine you to the 'polished shaft' *he* knows you can and will be.

"Sometimes it seems too much rain falls with never a break in the clouds. You have your testimony; no clouds or rain or flood has washed that away. Let it continue to be the *anchor to your soul.*"

Thinking about what he had written, I wondered if the Lord were still refining me. I stared at the ceiling while the contractions mounted. I thought back over the recent years—the trials and the triumphs—and wondered how far along I was in this refining process.

2
Among the Children of Men

In January of 1976 I joined The Church of Jesus Christ of Latter-day Saints, better known to me at the time as the Mormon Church. I never thought, as I was growing up, that I would ever be a member of the Mormon Church. Deep in my heart were feelings of hatred toward whites.

I had heard how the "all white" Mormon Church practiced white superiority by excluding blacks from its membership, and that they used revelation from God as the reason for doing so. Yet, after a difficult struggle with the Lord, the missionaries, and myself, it was impossible to cast off and deny what I knew in my heart to be true. I could neither erase nor overlook the feelings I had experienced when the missionaries shared their knowledge of the gospel with me. The Church of Jesus Christ of Latter-day Saints was indeed the true church of God upon this earth.

Even when I had come to know that the Church was true, I found it difficult to accept it into my life. Though I knew that all the bad things I had heard about the Church were not true, my family didn't share this knowledge. I was afraid! Afraid not only of the changes that had already begun to take place within me but also afraid to tell those I loved most of those changes, afraid that they would not understand or accept me anymore.

Despite all the feelings of fear I was unable to run from what I knew to be true—though I tried. Finally, I did what I had to do. I accepted the true gospel of Jesus Christ into my life even though it cost me the people I loved the most on this earth—my family.

Shortly after joining the Church I moved to Provo, Utah to find work and go to graduate school at BYU. Feeling a hunger and thirst for more knowledge in the gospel, I decided to take a few religion classes. But knowledge brought pain. One day as the instructor of my Gospel Principle and Practice class discussed a lesson on the priesthood, a note was passed to me. I opened it to read: "And Enoch beheld the residue of the people which were the sons of Adam and they were a mixture of all the seed of Adam save it was the seed of Cain, *for the seed of Cain were black and had not place among them.*" Seeing the last several words heavily underlined, I clearly understood the message. It was with great difficulty that I hid my shock and pain.

I was unable to forget that note and its possible validity as people frequently questioned me on why I joined the Church. What was I doing in Utah? Did I think I would find a black man in the Church to marry? One day as I was leaving a class a young man actually stopped me and asked me what it felt like to be black. His expression revealed his disgust that to be born black was the most repugnant and degrading thing that could happen to a person. Because I was proud of my color, I was able to answer him without the least bit of anger. "Like a beautiful daughter of God," I had said with a smile.

I was also made aware of some "cute" nigger jokes someone had told, but this soon stopped when people realized that I wouldn't tolerate them.

There were others who tried to show that they had my well-being at heart. Many made sure that I was aware of every black man in the vicinity. And if they knew one who was states away, they never hesitated to offer me his address. When a black was recruited to team sports—Church member or not—I was made aware of it. I was a daughter of Heavenly Father, but it seemed I was definitely not going to have a life of freedom and choice without the direction of many well-meaning people. It seemed they were saying we are brothers and sisters, but. . . .

At times the hardships of life and skin color seemed insurmountable. I found myself wondering why something that should bring happiness brought me the exact opposite. I felt labeled and stuck in a particular category and confined to it because of what was visible on the outside.

Despite all the hardships, though, my testimony of the truthfulness of the gospel was strong and undaunted. I knew the people in the Church were *striving* to become perfect, whereas the gospel was already perfect. I was grateful that I knew the difference, so that the actions of a few did not destroy my testimony. I was also grateful for the many who did bestow unconditional love; many whose names I never knew. I often thought about the time I was jogging around the track in the Smith Fieldhouse at BYU. As I came around for the third or fourth time a couple of junior high school boys standing off in a corner yelled, "How do you tell if a nigger has a black eye?" I don't know if they were directing their question to me, but they made sure I heard it. Though I had barely passed them, I immediately turned around. So did two men who had also been jogging. When they reached the boys ahead of me, one of them immediately asked for an apology. The boys protested, saying they weren't talking to me. The jogger told them it didn't matter, they should apologize to me and to them.

"Why?" one of the boys asked. "You're not black."

"Doesn't matter," the jogger said. "It still offended me."

The boys finally apologized. The joggers then asked them to leave, explaining to them that their type of attitude just wasn't appreciated there. I said nothing the whole time.

When the boys left, I turned and thanked the joggers.

"What's a brother for?" one of them said, and we began jogging again.

I found love and strength from many. I was always touched by the innocent love of children. I'll never forget the time I spoke in a fireside in Overton, Nevada. I was greeting people on the stand. I felt a tug on my skirt and looked down to see a little girl about three years old. I stooped down to say hello, and all she did was open her arms wide to hug me. Another time I was invited to have dinner with a Brother John Maestas and his family. He later told me he had worried about how his four-year-old son would respond to me. He said he had tried to educate his son about blacks, but he couldn't predict what the boy might say. When father and son came to pick me up for dinner, Brother Maestas introduced me to his son. Immediately the boy's eyes grew large. He said, "You're a pink lady." I was wearing a pink dress! I heard Brother Maestas take in a big breath when his son first began his sentence. Then I heard a big sigh of relief.

As time slowly passed, I made better adjustments to life in Utah and began to find strength in facing negative situations. But just when I thought that I had a good attitude about things, I let myself down. As I stood getting a drink of water I heard someone say, "Hello. My name is Chuck. What's yours?" I looked up and saw a tall, white guy standing nearby. He was smiling. But feeling exhausted and now perturbed with people who sought my first name and then asked the usual questions, I recoiled.

"My name is Shirley Temple Black. Yes, I am a Mormon. My father is Dallin Oaks. My mother is Camilla Kimball. Yes, Mother is older than Father and also has a different last name. Polygamy I suppose; nothing of great concern. My grandparents were Joseph and Emma Smith. I have a brother on a full-time mission." I paused then continued with the same tone of sarcasm. "Don't ask me how my brother got on a mission because yes, he's black like me." I turned and walked to the opposite side of the hall. I was sure that if I looked back, I would see an embarrassed face. Instead, when I turned, I found this man standing directly in front of me. Before I could gain my composure, he began talking.

"You didn't stick around for me to give you more information about myself," he said in a cool tone of voice. "As I said earlier, my name is Chuck. My father was the great Dr. Martin Luther King, Jr." He gave a proud bow with his head. I started to speak, but he held up his hand to silence me. "I have not finished, young lady," he said sternly. "So please honor me by letting me tell you my history as you did *without* my asking for it." He paused as he stood staring straight into my eyes, but showing no emotion. "Now, where was I before you so rudely interrupted me?" "Oh yeah, my mother's name is Harriet

Tubman. Like your parents, she too is older than my father and has a different last name, but I suppose it's because she could never legally marry father; something to do with the laws I believe. Anyway, nothing of great concern either. I can't tell you much about my grandparents, but I do have a black sister on a mission. It looks like we have a lot in common, *and* it looks as if you're the white sheep in your family, and I'm the black one in mine—or vice versa. Guess those are the breaks that some of us have to live with no matter how much we don't want to." He turned and walked away. I was totally embarrassed. What a rude awakening. I had prejudged someone's intent based on the actions of others.

I didn't see that young man in the weeks that followed, though I often found myself trying to recall what he had looked like. One Friday evening as I braided my hair, the phone rang. When I answered it, a male voice asked to speak to President Oaks.

"Sorry, you have the wrong number," I said.

Then he asked if President Oak's daughter was there.

My face went warm with embarrassment as I recalled the young man in the hall. "Just a moment and I'll see," I said, as I layed the phone down and pretended to go. I stood in my doorway, finding it hard to believe he was calling and wondering how he'd learned my real name and phone number. I returned to the phone. "Hello," I finally said, trying to change my voice.

"Who is this?" he asked.

"Mary," I said.

"Sorry," he said. "Must be a mistake. I asked to speak to President Oak's daughter, and if I recall correctly, her name is Shirley Temple Black. Do you think you could please see if *she's* there?"

"I'm sorry," I stammered out in frustration. "Just a moment and I'll see if she's here." Again I lay the phone down and walked to the door. I tried to think of a way to get the best of this situation. He had won the one in the hall, and I didn't want it to happen again. Unable to come up with anything, I returned to the phone.

"She can't come to the phone right now," I said, pausing for a few moments.

"Don't tell her about this call. I'll come over and surprise her." The phone clicked.

My blood pressure soared with fright as I replaced the phone on the receiver. And then, as if someone had stabbed me with a needle, I got busy. When I opened the door and saw his reaction to my appearance, the efforts paid off.

"I didn't know you were quite so heavy," he said, looking at me in a long, size 42 dress, every inch of it—including the long puffy sleeves—filled to the max. "Nor did I know you had blonde hair," he continued, still looking me over in shock.

"Guess that's life. Some of us get all the breaks."

We both had a good laugh, and a beautiful friendship began that evening.

Time found us taking long walks or bike rides together; walking downtown or up to BYU for an ice cream cone; attending ballgames, concerts, and other church or school activities. But the friendship didn't go without repercussions. We never held hands or showed in any way that there was anything more than friendship between us. But from seeing the negative reactions of people around us, anyone would have thought we were headed for the temple every time we went out together.

I think it was people's reaction to us that brought on a discussion one night as we sat outside. Chuck turned to me with a look that I recognized as his "something's-troubling-me look." I asked what was wrong. He asked me if I thought I could ever become serious about him.

"Depends on what you mean by serious."

"Serious as in boyfriend and girlfriend," he replied somewhat distraught.

"Well, considering you are a boy and I am a girl, I would say we are already boyfriend and girlfriend."

He didn't find my answer amusing and waited.

"I suppose I could," I finally said. "If you're asking that because you are white, I don't think it would bother me. I think

I've risen above skin color. I'm really happy with things the way they are, though. I don't plan to get serious with anyone until I know for certain that the Lord won't allow me to serve a full-time mission. As long as I have hope in my heart, I'll keep waiting. Could you ever get serious about me?"

"I could," he answered without hesitation, "But you don't want more, and I won't pressure you. I'm happy with the relationship we have."

"Chuck," I said, breaking an unbearable silence. "I would never want you or anyone like you to love me. I wouldn't let our relationship grow to the point of marriage, because only hurt could be the end result. I know what a temple marriage means to you and to every member of the Church. And I couldn't come between you and a temple marriage."

He pretended to laugh. "You know something," he said, "a girl in my ward asked me why I kept seeing you. She questioned what would happen if we became serious and I wanted to marry you. You know what I told her?"

I shook my head, almost afraid to hear it.

"I told her that if I became serious about you, and you about me, and if marriage was the next step, I would joyously make that step. I would marry you if you would have me. You see, Mary, I do want to marry in the temple. That's been a goal of mine ever since I was able to know and understand the purpose of the temple. Marrying you would mean I could not have that blessing. I know, as well as you know, that the Lord is going to make sure *all* his children have an opportunity to have his blessings, including the blessing of a temple marriage. And *all* includes *you.* I would be willing to wait with you and for you until your time for those blessings had come." I couldn't resist hugging him. After that day, although we continued to enjoy each other's friendship, we let marriage become a dead issue.

In June of 1978, the prophet received word from the Lord that the time had come to give "*all* worthy male members" the blessing of the priesthood. My heart was overwhelmed with joy. I had longed to serve a full-time mission since joining the Church but because of the restriction of the priesthood from my race I had not been able to do so. My day had finally come.

Three months after the revelation, I was on my way to serving that full-time mission. I had received a mission call from the Prophet of the Lord to serve in Texas. Although I did not really want to go to Texas and had sometimes begun to wonder if the Lord was trying to get rid of me permanently, it was only after being in the mission field and doing the Lord's work that I realized his wisdom in calling me to serve in that area of his vineyard. Though I went on a mission to share his gospel with others so they might receive his blessings, it was I who received the greatest blessings. As I dedicated myself to my Savior's work, I experienced a fulfillment in my life I had never known before. All too soon my full-time service for him came to an end.

When I returned to Provo and to BYU, I resumed life as I had left it—all except my relationship with Chuck. He had not told me while I was in the mission field that he was getting married. As I had thought back upon our friendship, my admiration for him had steadily grown. I had hoped to see him and continue the relationship when I returned from the mission field. When I heard of his marriage, I felt as if a part of me had slipped away. Nevertheless, I knew that my life and its future was in the Lord's hands, and he would care for me now as he had in times past.

Life slowly began to move forward again as I busied myself with graduate classes and began to teach English for the Indian Education Department at BYU. Life among members of the Church seemed markedly different after the revelation on the priesthood. People's attitudes seemed different. There seemed to be more of a color blindness.

I was different. The added blessings of going through the temple and on a mission brought deeper meaning and growth to my life. I felt better about myself, my worth as a human being and my capabilities as a daughter of Heavenly Father. I *knew* the Savior. I had felt his love, seen and understood His suffering. I *knew* the destiny I sought, and I made a firm commitment to myself that I would not allow the action and attitude of others to hinder me from reaching it.

3
What If?

On March 11, 1981, exactly one day short from being home from my mission for one year, a new chapter began in my life. I had a luncheon date with Ron Mortensen, a former student and a good friend from before my mission. I did not have to be at work until one o'clock, yet I had awakened earlier than planned. Unable to go back to sleep, I decided to go into the office and do some paperwork until time for my luncheon with Ron.

As I dressed, I thought about how happy life had been lately. I felt happy and complete with only one exception—I still did not have the sweet association of my family. No sooner had the thought come about my family than I suddenly felt depressed. Yet I knew in my heart that someday I would be with them again.

By the time I finished dressing and knelt in prayer, the depression had increased. Still puzzled as to why, I tried to pray, but as I said Heavenly Father's name, my eyes grew wet. "This is ridiculous," I wanted to say aloud, but the words were muffled by sobs. I couldn't understand what was happening nor why. I really felt silly there crying, especially when I noticed my little dog Snotzi staring at me. I tried to laugh, but no sound came. Succumbing to the tears, I let myself cry until my body felt totally drained. As I went to wash my face, a feeling of serenity filled me. I also felt a strangeness, an emptiness I could not explain.

After the lunch with Ron, I was late for work and half ran back to the office. "Hey, Mary, when are we going to play racquetball?" I turned to see somebody who looked as though he had forgotten to shave that morning. Also, the way he was dressed left a lot to be desired.

"Are you talking to me?" I asked quickly, still trying to get to work.

"Yes, I am," he said, ignoring my impatience. Then he repeated, "When are we going to play racquetball?"

I tried to recall who he was and when I had made a date with him to play racquetball. Apparently noticing my confusion, he explained he had been at one of my firesides and that the man who had introduced me said that I was a great racquetball player and would enjoy a good challenge. "So I am here to challenge you."

"Oh?" Looking at him, despite my love for racquetball, I found myself regretting he had heard the introduction. "Are you any good?"

"I'm pretty good; good enough to beat you."

"Well, I doubt if you're *that* good," I retaliated. "So far, I know only one person who can truly beat me, and that's Elder Hartman Rector, Jr.; but eventually I'll be able to spot him ten points and still beat him." I paused. "I'll tell you what. I'll do the same for you."

"First you have to get ten points before you can spot me ten, and I doubt if you'll get one unless I give it to you," he said.

I wasn't sure if he was teasing. As we talked a little longer, I was sure he wasn't.

I didn't know when I would be able to play a game, so I gave him my number to arrange it later. We decided right then, however, that the loser would have to buy dinner.

"By the way, in case you want to know who'll be beating you (as if sure he would win), my name is John Eyre. Don't sweat the cost of dinner too much. I'll choose something inexpensive." He turned and walked off.

I tried to get another look at him. As he walked away, he was looking down at the slip of paper, where I had written my phone number. A strange feeling gripped me.

When he called a few nights later, we were able to schedule a date to play in two weeks. As the date grew nearer and my work seemed to pile up, I found myself wishing I had not made the date at all. I called BYU information and got his number. I planned to call him and cancel, but I never got around to doing it. After we played, I knew I should have. He was an excellent player! The game was long and strenuous, but he emerged the victor.

To protect my pride, at dinner I told him not to feel too proud. "I played left-handed," I said with a smirk. All the life drained out of him. "But then, I'm left-handed," I added.

At first I wasn't sure he thought it was funny, but in a moment we both started laughing. He was obviously relieved.

As we began to talk I was surprised at how easy our conversation was; how readily we shared things about our lives, especially our feelings about the gospel and about important experiences we'd had because of it. Dinner came and ended much too soon. Before long our evening together and our discussion of life had come to an end. When he asked me out for the following night, I didn't hesitate to accept, even though I was already booked up. In my mind I was already formulating excuses to break the other. I felt drawn to him, and the feeling was mystifying and exciting.

Time couldn't tick away fast enough the next day. I kept reminiscing back to the first day he had confronted me on campus and how unimpressed I had been with him. I thought about dinner and how relaxed and down to earth we had been in our conversations. I wanted to see him, to be with him, to listen to him, talk to him, laugh with him.

When our date had come and gone, I was better able to understand the feelings inside me. John showed the same great qualities I had so admired in Chuck. We began spending some time together almost every day following that night. There was always so much to talk about, so many costless things to do. Though I had heard it said many times that two people have more in common when they have the same background, we were both very thankful that ours were different—so extremely different! There was so much about our separate worlds that we were able to share with each other. The surprises seemed endless and the growth constant. And then there was the common bond we shared—a love for our Savior and his true gospel. With so much between us to appreciate, it was not long before the relationship bloomed.

I was growing to like John, and I knew it. In a sense, the thought frightened me. I didn't know if I wanted to get serious. If I did, what hassles would it create? My nights became restless as I thought about him and how our relationship would have to end. The more time we spent together, the more worried I became. I found myself going through almost the same ordeal I had gone through when the missionaries had shared the true gospel of Christ with me—except that this time I could pray, whereas before I had not, even believed, there was a God to pray to.

I knew I had to face the turmoil that was steadily building inside of me. I must eventually answer the pounding question of "What if this relationship grows to a question of marriage?" I desperately wanted to feel that I was capable of an unconditional love that could extend beyond the boundaries of friendship, yet from all that I had heard from others, to feel this kind of love was wrong in the eyes of the Lord if the loved one was of a different race. Statements people made seemed especially geared toward love between whites and blacks. I felt lost. It was hard to understand how I could ever know the fullness of the Savior's love if I had to place a condition on my own. It was a contradiction that said, "Okay, you may like this person, but you cannot love him in the eternal sense unless he's of your race." It all seemed so contrary to the love of the Savior. If he was no respecter of persons, why must I be?

I decided that instead of accepting what people told me I would look for information on the issue of interracial marriage. I didn't want to paralyze my thinking and growth by the "hearsay" of others.

Being unable to find any concrete information on the issue, I decided to go directly to those whom everyone declared as the source: the apostle and the Prophet. I made various appointments with different brethren in Salt Lake City. I decided it was best to talk to more than one to see if their answers correlated. I met first with Elder Hartman Rector, Jr., then with Elders Dean L. Larsen, LeGrand Richards, and finally with the Prophet. Their answers were the same.

I don't know if President Kimball knew the turmoil I had suffered, but as I expressed to him my sincere desire to know the Lord's will on interracial marriage, tears slowly rolled down his face. Reaching out, he gently embraced me as one would a delicate and small child. Then he quietly but emphatically whispered, "My child, it is not wrong. It is not wrong. The only reason we counsel against it is because of the problems the *children* could face. As far as it's being incompatible with the Lord's gospel, or with your Father in Heaven, it is not." He paused, still looking into my eyes. I felt that he saw into my soul. Then with another brief embrace he uttered, "Be of good cheer; the Lord loves you dearly."

As I walked down the steps of the Church Administration Building that day, I felt as if the arms of the Prophet were still around me. Once I reached that last step I turned to look back at the building, the door, the Prophet still inside. No longer did I carry the burdens of frustration.

With time steadily passing John and I progressed from "I really like you" to "I really care." One day I looked at all the flowers he had given me (though they had long ago dried away to nothing, they remained permanent fixtures). Every note he had given me had been read and reread. I couldn't deny how special and meaningful the relationship was. I then asked myself: "Am I falling in love with him?" The answer did not bring frustration but a quiet smile of happiness.

John asked me if I would go home with him when the school year ended. Though apprehensive, I told him I would. I knew his mother's letters to him had expressed concern about our relationship and what could eventually come of it. I was also aware of his grandmother's feelings, which weren't good at all. Despite how strong and secure I felt about myself, I did not feel ready to go through any hassles with anyone, especially John's family.

A couple of weeks before we were to leave for his home, I wrote to his mother. I expressed to her how much I wanted to meet her, but how many anxieties I felt as well. I told her how much John and I had come to mean to each other. I asked her to trust us to make the right decision.

> "I do ask you to please not prejudge me and my worthiness of your son's devotion and love because of what your eyes may first see. Give me a chance as a person—a daughter of God—and maybe in time you will come to see, understand, and perhaps feel what John already feels."

I don't recall much about the drive to John's home. Most of the way I sat deep in thought—worried about what awaited me. As anxiety built, I recalled another anxious time. I had felt similar feelings the day I faced Daddy after an embarrassing incident with him. I had been a cheerleader since seventh grade, a cheerleader who could attend home and away games only if a family member or two could accompany us. In tenth grade I decided to remain after a game for a dance that was to be held later that night. I waited for at least an hour after the dance had started before coming out, feeling certain my brothers had left. Taking a careful look around the gym and seeing my brothers were gone, I relaxed and proceeded out onto the dance floor. It never occurred to me that Daddy would come looking for me. I assumed he would send my brothers back, and by the time they returned I would have danced a few dances. I felt whatever punishment Daddy gave me would be worth the defiance. Midway through a song I was dancing to, I felt someone grasp hold of the back of the sweater I was wearing in a manner that I knew was not a joke nor an accident. As the force of the grip began to draw me backwards off the dance floor, I protested. But judging by the power of the pull, I knew it was Daddy. Daddy was a man of few words, and that night he didn't bother expressing any. I simply hid my face in shame and hoped for the moment to end soon. The defiance wasn't worth the humiliation his dragging me out had cost.

We arrived at John's home by early afternoon. As we stopped, a lady going across the street turned and started back in our direction.

"That's my mom," John said, and he got out of the car and hugged her. As I sat waiting for him to open my door, I glanced at her. She stood watching him come around to my side of the car. She was not smiling. My heart sank.

"Well here goes," I thought as I got out of the car. I spoke a greeting to her, but wasn't sure if she returned one. When John introduced us, I again said hello. She acknowledged with a smile. I heard myself let go of a big sigh of relief.

We had anticipated spending our summer together, but in early June John got an internship with Xerox in New York. Before school had ended, he had written them a letter about coming, but we both had hoped that he wouldn't get the position. The news put a damper on things. After sitting and saying very little to each other all evening, we went ouside for a late walk. Though it began to rain, we walked for hours, grateful for the storm and the refreshing feeling it brought. Still we didn't say much as we walked hand in hand. Every so often we gave one another a squeeze of the palm to say, "I love you."

Hours later we came back to the apartment, both soaked from the rain. Once inside John took my hand, and with a look of sadness in his eyes said, "I don't know how to say this." His voice broke as he swallowed hard. I wasn't sure why he was so sad, but I got the feeling something horrible was about to happen. As if searching for words, he looked into my eyes and for a moment said nothing.

"I'm not sure what or how to say this, so here goes," he said again, sounding a bit nervous. "I have truly enjoyed being with you, Mary, and I want you at my side as you are now for all eternity."

"Like this?" I protested in horror as I wiped the rain from my face, knowing my hair hung like a lump of grass. Then it hit me exactly what he was saying, and my mouth dropped open.

"Will you marry me?" he asked. His hand touched my face. I stared at him in shock but managed to nod my head "yes." When I was finally able to get myself together, I told him it didn't sound real and to please do it over. He did, this time getting down on his knees. Smiling happily, I told him I would be honored to marry him. We then knelt in prayer to our Father in Heaven for his approval and acceptance of the decision we had made.

The next few days we made plans for the future. Since John would be going through Chicago on his way to Rochester, New York and since Mama was living with one of my brothers there, we decided to introduce John to Mama to get her approval.

4
To Be Home Again

Early one Thursday morning John picked me up, and we began the long, apprehensive drive to Chicago. We were only going to have one night there, since John had to be in Rochester by a certain date and I had obligations in Utah. Dad Strong had given us both a blessing before we left, which gave me a great deal of comfort, yet I wished as we drove that by some miracle I would awaken and find the whole trip behind me—a dream.

Wanting to give John insight about my brothers that were living in Chicago in case we encountered them, I briefed him on some of their habits and hobbies when I had lived at home.

"Louise is our greatest hope for survival," I said to him. "She talks really fast but please don't ask her to repeat anything. She just might take offense, and I would feel sorry for you if she did." He nodded his head with understading. "Then there's Ernie. He loves cars, especially fast ones, and since you're going to be a car designer one day you two should have plenty to talk about—if you stay alive long enough." Again he nodded. "Frank lives in Chicago, too, and he loves photography. So do you, so there's a door that can open to discussion." He approved as he checked to make sure he had his camera. "Charles loves trucks and since you spent a summer driving one, if he gives you a chance—before he tries to kill you—yell quickly that you know a lot about trucks—even if you don't. At least that might lead to a discussion." I continued, "Roy loves basketball. I would definitely advise you *NOT* to play against him. He goes for blood, and if you score a basket against him or foul him, you might as well give up any hope of living." John commented that he wasn't too fond of basketball so he probably wouldn't bother playing Roy a game. I agreed that his decision was a good one. "Curtis loves talking about black history. Try not to get involved in a conversation with him. He loves ripping people to shreds and would especially love to rip you apart." He nodded with agreement. "Bobby loves. . . ."

"Hold it," John said, the sweat on his forehead clearly visible. "I doubt if I'll live long enough to use any of this information."

"That was going to be my concluding point, but since you have already made that brilliant conclusion, let me warn you that if you do live long enough to use it, don't confuse who likes what because that would infuriate them. The one thing I didn't tell you is that they all love guns, knives, and baseball bats." Though I had hoped to do all this humorously, neither of us laughed; the reality of it was too intense.

The closer we got to Chicago, the less we talked. A few times I glanced over at John, wanting to give him comfort, but my fear made it difficult to think of something positive to say. I finally reached into the back seat and got my journal.

"I still find it hard to believe that God has blessed me with such a good, strong man for an eternal mate," I wrote. "What can I say or how do I explain to you, dear journal, why we are headed to a situation we both fear?" Pausing, I sat thinking about Mama and how each time she went into labor with a child, she would say the Twenty-third Psalm, once completely through. Then over and over she would repeat: "and yeah, though I walk through the valley of shadow of death, I will fear no evil for thou art with me." Putting my journal away, I silently said the Twenty-third Psalm, seeking the comfort of the Lord as we neared Chicago.

It was late evening by the time we arrived in the Chicago area. With his arm resting out the window, John seemed relaxed and composed as we drove slowly searching for Louise's house. The evening was very muggy, and people sat outside on their porches or on old beat-up cars hoping to feel a breeze.

As we drove down the street, everyone stared. Conversations

seemed to halt abruptly. Because the stares were becoming glares of anger, I asked John to take his arm inside the car. He asked why. I tried to explain that his relaxed manner could be construed as cockiness. Some black guy might just grab his arm and rip it off.

John had barely drawn in his arm when we passed a car crowded with blacks. Most of them were sitting on the hood. As we drove by, they turned, pointed to John and sneered. "Honky!" one of them yelled.

The others joined in with crude comments, but we drove quickly out of range. Though we could not understand the words clearly, we knew they weren't welcoming remarks. I looked at John and was scared. He was smiling!

"What have you got to smile about?" I snapped at him. "Here I sit scared sick, and you sit there smiling. I see nothing to smile about, and I'm black. So please let me in on the joke."

He quickly turned to me. When I saw the look in his eyes I felt awful for snapping at him.

"I've wanted to do this for so long," he said. His voice shook with sincere emotion as if this were the greatest thing to ever happen to him.

"What?" I asked, stunned by his remarks.

"I don't mean I have always wanted a situation like ours," he said. "I don't want to upset these people or feel their anger toward me. I mean, I have always wanted to see this part of Chicago. I worked one summer for Amtrak on the route from Oakland to Chicago. Many of the evenings we spent overnight here I would take the railtrain and ride downtown. The train always went through the black areas, and as it did I could see blacks sitting outside as they are today: their children playing, radios blasting, old clothes hanging on the porch or clotheslines. I just wanted to get off the train and talk to them, to be in their midst and see how they lived. And today. . . ." He gave a heavy sigh, ". . . today I'm actually here, and I feel thankful. I feel as though the Lord has given me a blessing I never took the time to ask for."

I was amazed at the tone of John's calm reflection. I wanted to understand what he was feeling, but my fear was too great. Instead, I prayed that we would soon find Louise's house.

Just when I began to wonder if the address was correct, John saw it: a two-story building very much in need of paint. For a moment, as I glanced at the windows, I was reminded of the old house I had grown up in—though this one was larger.

Hearing some children across the street yelling, "Hey, white boy." I came out of my daze. We looked at each other and smiled (or tried to). John's face showed little or no worry at all. He reached to give me a hug, but fearing what "the neighbors might think," I quickly turned away, telling him we had best get inside.

The children began yelling again, calling John names, asking him what he was doing there. But John just smiled and waved to them.

We rang and rang the doorbell to Louise's house, but no one came to the door. "Oh Lord," I prayed silently. "What do we do now?" I frantically rang the doorbell again and again. Acutely aware of stares, I felt it best to go back and get in the car. As we started back three little boys came running and asked us who we were. When we told them, they stared.

"Louise is our mother," one of them said.

Relief swept through me. "Mama and Grandma went to a revival at church."

"They won't be home till late."

I asked them if Louise had received my letter telling her we were coming.

"No," the oldest one said.

"Yes," the smallest one said.

"I don't know," the middle child admitted.

The one that said "no" and appeared to be the oldest told us Louise would want us to wait at Ernie's until she came home. The one who had said she *did* get the letter said she wanted us to stay there. The one who didn't know about the letter said he didn't know what we were to do.

I looked to John for his decision.

"Let's go over to Ernie's," he said, causing me to nearly choke. "John, are you sick?" I asked him, finding it hard to believe what I had heard. He had better have a profound reason for such a plan.

"Okay," the littlest one said. "I'll go wif you to show you how to git there."

Before I could say anything he and John had marched off to the car.

"Ma dear gon whip you," the oldest one said.

"Not," the little one with John said.

"You see, " the oldest one said, sounding pretty sure of himself.

"I be back 'fore she gits home," the littlest one said impatiently waiting for John to unlock the car.

"I still tell on you," the older one yelled.

"Me, tell her, too," the middle child joined in.

"So! Ma dear won't mine; these our folks!" the littlest child squeaked inside the car. He looked at them and made a face.

I told them we would be back soon, and if Louise came, to be sure to let her know where we had gone.

It was evident as I got in the car that John had already made a friend. The little boy was talking a blue streak. John was able to interrupt long enough to learn that his name was Terrace. I wanted to convince John that perhaps going to Ernie's wasn't such a good idea, but he and Terrace didn't allow me to get a word in.

"I can roll my belly," Terrace said proudly as he started to stand.

"Not now, Terrace." John said. "Wait until we get to Ernie's."

Instead of taking us to Ernie's house, Terrace directed us to a car shop Ernie owned. I thought John would park out front, but there was a door used for driving inside and he did exactly that. As we pulled inside we could see two of my brothers—Ernie and Charles—seated directly ahead of us. They sat eating. At least they were eating before they saw us. If stares could kill, we would have been dead before John could have turned off the ignition.

I didn't realize my heart was pounding so loudly until Terrace asked me what was that noise. I was about to tell John

"Let's get out of here," but he was already out of the car. As he got out he both spoke and waved a hello. John ignored my brother's lack of response as he opened my door. Then he turned to them and asked, "What are you eating?"

They said nothing.

"We're starving," he said. My stomach collapsed. I quickly realized we had not stopped to eat that day, but I felt suddenly full. It wasn't food; it was fear.

After John let me out, he walked over to where they sat. He again said hello and introduced himself, extending a hand. Ernie's wife was the only one who responded. John repeated his earlier remark about being hungry. Again only Ernie's wife said anything. "Well," she said, "do you want half my sandwich?"

Before John could answer she had divided it in half, and she handed part of it to him. I stood the whole time not saying a word.

"You hungry?" Ernie asked me. I nodded my head, close to tears. I wanted so much to hug him and tell how good it felt at that moment to see him again. He was much heavier now, but his facial features seemed unchanged by time. Timidly I reached for the sandwich he offered. At that moment Charles got up and walked away. Seeing him do this really broke my heart. I so much wanted—and needed—their love. I kept my eyes on Charles, afraid he might try to do something to harm us. I kept glancing to see if he were getting a weapon. My heart was pounding so hard I was sure everyone could hear it.

Ernie's wife began talking. She asked how the weather was when we left. John responded with exuberance. Ernie asked if we wanted more to eat. Realizing I had not eaten what he had given me, I quickly gulped it down so that I could say yes, anxious to show need and gratitude. John also said "Sure."

Ernie yelled over at Charles and asked if he would go get us some food. At first I thought Charles hadn't heard as he continued doing what he was doing, keeping his back to us.

"I 'spose I can, man," he finally said halfheartedly.

I was about to tell him he didn't have to, that we could wait, but John was already saying, "Great."

"What y'all want?" Charles asked a few minutes later, not looking at either of us.

"Whatever you were eating," John said.

"That's okay with me, too," I uttered weakly.

"Let me give you some money," John said, reaching in his pocket.

"Forget it," Charles said as he started walking off.

"No," John said. "I can pay for it. Besides, I'd like a cold drink, too."

But Charles continued on his way, ignoring John, never breaking his stride.

"Charles. . . ," John said and was about to insist on giving him the money. "John," I said in a low voice, gritting my teeth.

By the time Charles returned, John and Ernie were discussing cars. Charles looked disturbed as they talked, but said nothing. When Ernie was called to the phone, John walked over to Charles who was working on a car. I wasn't sure what John said, but I did hear the word "truck." He had remembered who liked what.

When it came time for Ernie to close the shop, he suggested we leave the car there for the night, explaining to John that if he left it outside, he might find a pile of ashes in the morning. I felt grateful for Ernie's concern. Not knowing where we should go, I asked Ernie.

"Guess you can come to our place 'til Louise comes," he said, though he didn't sound the least bit enthusiastic.

No one said very much while we waited for Louise. But soon three more of my brothers arrived, and they began to talk and laugh among themselves. Someone had a camera and started taking pictures. When they went to take one of John, he grabbed a still somewhat indifferent Charles and pulled him into the picture with him. The laughter stopped. Charles looked at John with shrill anger as the room went dead with silence.

"Smile," John said, poking Charles in the side and completely ignoring Charles' reaction and the stillness of the room. "I don't want you to make me look bad." The camera clicked, and John yelled for a retake, saying they weren't ready.

He then started pulling others into the picture. Before long, Charles joined in to help him. Laughter started breaking the silence. John and Charles were both laughing.

Everything was still going smoothing when Mama and Louise walked in. At first I wasn't sure who Mama was. The lady that stood before me had sunken, hollow cheeks. Her eyelids looked swollen, making her eyes almost impossible to see. Her skin looked dry and drained of life. When she spoke to me, the voice lacked stamina and the words were brittle, though she barely uttered them. I quickly glanced down at the rest of her. The dress she had on looked as though all the life had been washed out of it. The patterns and color were faded. I was about to look at her shoes, when a lump entered my throat. I had seen that dress before! Mama must have sensed my recognition of it, for when I looked at her, a smile crossed her face and tears filled her eyes.

"Oh, Mama," I said, my own tears starting to fall. I don't know how long we stood there embracing. I feared that if I let go, I would never be able to hold her again. Two of my brothers placed their hands on Mama's shoulders. I didn't want them to take her from me and pulled her closer.

"Frances," one said to me, "her legs have given out. We need to sit her down." It wasn't until I started to loosen my hold on Mama did I realize that I had been supporting her weight. I watched as they carried her frail and fragile body to a chair. Her eyes never left mine. As my brothers eased Mama down into the chair, I felt so proud of her. She had known I was coming, and despite how hot and muggy it was, she had worn the dress I had sent her my first Christmas away from home. Seeing her with it on now, I recalled that she had also worn it to Daddy's funeral for me.

As if knowing what I was thinking at that moment, Louise looked at me and said, "Maybe you can tell Mama to throw that dress away now. People must think it's the only one she has."

"Yea," Charles said. "It could be a hundred and ten degrees, and she'll have it on."

Mama, still looking at me, smiled as she pulled out an old

rag and wiped tears from her eyes.

John walked over and knelt in front of her. Because everyone in the room was talking and laughing now, I was unable to hear what he said. She responded and they suddenly hugged. Again the room seemed quiet. I looked around watching everyone. As I did, I saw Roy. He stood in the doorway observing John and Mama. With an angry look on his face, he turned and disappeared. I looked back at John and Mama, knowing they had not seen Roy. Tears were flowing down Mama's cheeks. When John turned to come over to me, I saw he also had tears in his eyes.

The plan was that we were to stay overnight with Louise. Louise seemed businesslike as we piled into her car. Before leaving she told us she had forgotten something at Ernie's. We waited while she went inside. She was gone for a long time and did not bring anything with her when she returned.

"Louise?" I hesitated.

She only looked at me.

"Did Ernie or any of them say anything to you about John and me when you went back inside to talk to them?"

Louise looked wary. She turned without an answer to walk out of the room. But then she stopped. She turned to me and said in a level tone, "I went back to tell them I was sorry."

I was quiet.

"When I told them y'all were coming, they said I was to make sure you stayed your distance from them. I promised them I would, but you came sooner than I thought you would, and then Terrace took you exactly where you weren't wanted."

"I'm sorry, Louise," I said. "I didn't mean to get you into trouble. I wouldn't do that to you. We really appreciate your letting us come. Is that all they had to say?"

"They said you are different."

"Is that all they said?" I asked, afraid to ask if the difference they talked about was good or bad.

"I don't think you want to hear the rest. It isn't nice." She started toward the door then stopped as if thinking of something else to say. After a few seconds she turned quickly toward me, paused again, then walked over and gave me a hug. "That was for Mama," she said. She then turned and left the room even though I called her name.

I sat on the bed after Louise left the room and thought about what she had said. I knew I was different from the way I had been when I was home. I felt different but would they ever give me a chance to tell them what the gospel was all about—how it could literally change a person and that such a change had happened to me? Would they ever understand? I was grateful they saw that I was different—hopefully for the better. Yet I couldn't help wondering what they thought I would be like. I felt lonely at that moment, and I ached to feel their love. I reflected over the time they had been teasing me about being skinny and ugly and that a few days later a neighbor boy who had seen their teasing decided to call me "ugly," too. My brother Roy nearly broke that boy's jaw with a punch. "Nobody calls our sister ugly," he said as he placed a protective arm around me. The boy tried to tell Roy he was just teasing me, but Roy punched him again and told him that only family could tease like that, and he wasn't family.

As I stared at myself in a mirror, I thought I looked old, tired, and weak. I wanted desperately to be a child again. Feeling sobs build in my throat, I succumbed to them and thought about times when I was home with my family—close times—times when we all pulled and suffered together, times we laughed, times we cried, times we talked, times we listened, times when we were a *family.*

Louise came in the next morning as I was gathering my things to leave. When she walked in, we looked at each other, but neither said a word.

"I love you, Louise," I said, breaking the silence.

She looked at me for a long moment. I tried understanding the look in her eyes but couldn't. Finally she said, "You were always different. You wanted an education and cried when you couldn't go to school. Even when there was work we could do to get money, you went to school. High school wasn't enough; you wanted to go to college, too. You wanted to be equal. You talked against whites—and God. You left home all by yourself; you, you, you. I have wondered if you were meant to be in our family or just got dropped off at the wrong house." She didn't sound bitter; she sounded both happy and sad for me.

"I wanted all those things, but I never thought I would lose y'all in seeking to accomplish them," I said, more to myself than to her. "I love y'all, Louise. Please don't exclude me. Please don't," I pleaded as I touched her arm. She took a step back from me and my touch as she stared at the floor.

"Mama always taught us that the Lord would provide. I teach my children that, too, and I have also added to that: There is a time and season for all things, even for families to get back together," she said and left the room.

I took my time getting things together, hoping Louise would return. "You goin?" a voice behind me said. I turned to find Terrace standing in my doorway. I smiled and walked over to him. I looked into his eyes. "Do you like John?"

He didn't answer right away. Instead he stood with one eye closed as if thinking about it. "Um huh," he finally said but with a frown, as if it were hard to say, "But he white, Frances."

"Is that okay?" I asked, wondering if that was why he frowned.

"I 'spose so. I can roll my belly," he quickly said and began rolling it.

"Terrace, you love me?" I asked, ignoring his rolling stomach.

"You like white people," he said with disapproval.

"Terrace, I like people, all people. People are. . . ."

"Terrace," Louise yelled for him from the other room before I could finish.

Louise, her husband, and Terrace drove us to Ernie's shop so John could get the car. Terrace wanted to show John he could roll his stomach, but Louise told him she would spank him if he did, so he rode in silence but looked angry. The two people who did talk were Louise's husband and John. Her husband had served in the military and now worked in a practically all-white situation. He had no problem with John being white. A couple of times I looked over at Louise, who sat with her eyes closed. I think she was praying. When we got to Ernie's shop, we found Mama, Charles, and Ernie and his wife waiting for us. Charles had even washed and waxed the car for us. After John thanked him, a moment of subdued silence filled the shop. Small talk started and then we began saying our goodbyes.

Louise was the first. To my surprise she hugged John as she said goodbye. Mama hugged him and started crying as she expressed her joy in our coming and her sorrow in our leaving. Ernie said, "Take care, man," while Charles added a "Yeah, do that, will you?" as he gave John a handshake. When John had finished his goodbyes, I started mine. Louise was first again. She didn't hesitate in hugging me.

"This time it's from me," she whispered.

Again I said, "I love you, Louise."

"I know," she whispered. "I know you do; we all know you do."

I looked at Ernie and waited. Feeling he wouldn't, I quickly threw my arms around him. At first there was no response. Then I felt a hand on my back.

It wasn't until I went to hug Charles that I saw Roy standing off in the distance, again observing all that was happening. Charles, like Ernie, didn't say anything. I looked back over where Roy had been and he had moved in closer. Then he walked over to where we all stood and looked straight in John's eyes as if staring right through him. No one moved nor said a word. I started praying, feeling certain trouble was about to start.

"Take care of her, man," Roy finally said. His words were cold, like a warning. His eyes were penetrating. John assured him he would as he extended his hand to Roy. My heart stopped beating in anticipation. Looking as if he were going to ignore John's hand, Roy finally extended his. A *FIRST* for Roy, and it said more to me than any words he could have said or failed to say.

I was still staring at them all in astonishment when Roy turned and looked at me.

"Goodbye, Frances," he said, making it sound final. I felt

life drain out of me. Mama walked over, took me in her arms as if I were a little girl and started to cry. She had understood, as I had, what Roy was saying. John took my hand and said we had best get started for the airport. We all tried saying a cheery goodbye as we drove off. It wasn't until we were driving away that I noticed something in my hand. Mama had placed there the old rag she had used for her tears.

John seemed overwhelmed with gratitude at how well he had been treated. Frankly, so was I. He suggested we find a place to stop and have a prayer to thank Heavenly Father for taking care of us. I felt the same, knowing that there were doors the Lord had opened. In time, I knew that he—even more than I—would open them even wider.

5
Yesterdays

Saying goodbye to John in Chicago prior to our three month separation was extremely difficult. As difficult as saying goodbye to my family. Being with my family again had not been like the close times we had shared when we grew up, but I was grateful for having seen some of their faces again, heard their voices, felt their touch. I had so often prayed for a chance to see them once more, but never felt quite sure if it would ever happen.

As the plane lifted into the sky from the Chicago's O'Hare Airport en route to Salt Lake City, my heart tore into a million pieces. As I stared out the window, through my tears I could see the images of houses—millions of them. Knowing that in one of them was my mama, I silently said goodbye to her again. There still were so many things in my heart that I wished I had said to her. Most of all, I wanted to feel her arms around me again, the very arms I so often rejected as a child.

I noticed all the traffic moving in different directions. Though I knew it was impossible, I still tried to find John's car among them. I was so proud of how he had handled himself, for the way he never showed any fear, though I knew it was there. I prayed for his safety as he traveled on to Rochester, New York and hoped he would remember to read Philemon 4 at the end of each day.

I wondered what my brothers had said after we left. What had been their feelings about John? I felt that they had been impressed, even touched by his sincerity. Perhaps now they could begin to feel that maybe there was at least one half-way good white person on the earth. But then as I recalled the time a white man had helped Roy when Roy's car had broken down in a strange town, I knew it was possible that their impression had not changed at all. Though I could tell Roy had been grateful and touched by all the help the white guy had given him, he never once verbally expressed it. "A white is a white, and you can't trust any of them" was a fact with them that seemed unchangeable.

Resting my head against the seat, I continued thinking about my brothers. I tried to recall when their bitterness toward whites had started. Though I knew that they weren't born with their hatred, it certainly seemed that way. As far back as I could recall, they had always hated whites. Roy was the one we had all considered the meanest; yet, he was also the one we thought would be a preacher. He was the one who would always gather us younger ones together to play church. We would gather around the old Roy-made pulpit and let him deliver us a sermon. He generally preached the story of Job, except that Job was a black man named "Smart Joe." All Smart Joe's afflictions were brought upon him by a white man who wanted Smart Joe to say "yes sir" and "no sir," both of which Smart Joe refused to do. We would cheer and clap our hands as Smart Joe endured the many afflictions placed upon him. The cheering mounted each time Smart Joe would look the white man in the eyes and say, "I's still ain't gon say it. Now or ever!" Roy always pounded the old pulpit hard. Then he ended the sermon by telling us that we *had* to be like Smart Joe and that we *had* to go a step further. We were not to take "no stuff off them at all. Not to let 'em push us around." By the end of the sermon we were jumping up and down shouting that we would be tough. Louise shouted the loudest—not with approval, but with an effort to quiet us down. She would always yell for us to "sing a hymn."

Louise was a lot like Mama, though she would get angry whenever we made a comparison. She wanted so much to be included in things, and she knew most of us disapproved of the way Mama felt. She was the only one who ever tried to get Roy to preach a different sermon other than the "Smart Joe" one. But we always voted in favor of it. She would sneak off and tell Mama whenever we were saying bad things about whites, which made Mama get after us. She was also the one who would tell Mama whenever we didn't close our eyes when Mama was praying. I could never understand how she knew whose eyes were open; she always assured Mama hers were closed. She was the one Mama never had to get after to go to church; she always got up on Sundays ready to go. As I thought about her now, I realized that I had never heard her say a mean thing to Mama; never heard her disagree with her—at least not so Mama could hear. She had struggled to be accepted both by us and by Mama, and had somehow managed it.

I tried to recall when I had first realized Ernie's hatred, but it just seemed as if his, too, had always been there. The time I had felt his strongest hatred was when his oldest daughter had been sick. Ernie had fallen in love at fifteen and married. They couldn't afford a place of their own so they had crowded in with us. One long hard winter when his daughter was two years old, she had come down with a serious illness. Mama had tried different home remedies but nothing helped, and Ernie's daughter grew worse. After a week, it was evident that the baby had to see a doctor. We tried borrowing money from neighbors, but the winter had everyone struggling to make ends meet. One morning, when the baby was burning up with fever, Ernie wrapped her up securely in old pieces of quilts. With one of Daddy's old sweaters on he walked into town to find a doctor, though he didn't have a penny. By late evening he returned, the baby still in his arms and tears glittering down his cheeks. Without any money, he had been unable to get a doctor to see him. He handed the baby to Mama and went back outside. I had never seen Ernie cry before, and it scared me. That night I was awakened by more crying, this time actually more like screaming. Seeing a dim light on in the next room, I jumped out of bed to see what was going on. I accidently kicked my sister Brenda in the stomach as I left. Although she screamed, I never stopped to apologize. I was listening to the screams coming from the other room. When I entered the room, I saw Mama huddled close to the stove with Ernie's baby still in her arms, still wrapped as she had been when Ernie had returned with her earlier. Now, however, the baby's face was clearly visible. Mama was staring down at her and crying, but her cries weren't the ones I had heard. Outside, Ernie's crying pierced through the fierce blowing wind and penetrated clearly inside. His baby had died. When Daddy saw me standing just inside the room shivering, he ordered me back to bed, told me to go back to sleep. But sleep was impossible. I lay listening to Ernie cry. Between sobs he swore many terrible and bitter things against whites in a way that I had never heard. Although I had never heard him say anything nice about whites before his baby died, I definitely never heard him say anything nice afterwards. Before, he would laugh when jokes were told about them, but now jokes only brought a haunting look of anger to his eyes. Reflecting over that incident made me even more grateful for the way things had gone between John and Ernie.

Then my thoughts turned to Charles. He had wanted to be a judge, so we often played court. He took great joy in sentencing us when we pretended to be white. It did not matter if the white person was the victim or not, Charles always sentenced him to life and would add, "Throw away the key once this honky is locked behind bars." Court was fun, and we all looked forward to playing it. Sometimes, though, the fun was cut short when Mama found out—thanks to Louise. It bothered Mama to see us having so much joy cleansing society of white people. Once when she made us stop, I angrily jumped to my feet and shouted, "Judge, how about sentencing this lady so we can be rid of her, too!"

Mama walked over and stood directly in front of me and quietly asked, "And what would you have thim do to me, child?"

Now, and many times since that time, I have wished I would have said, "Nothing, Mama." Instead, I had looked at her and said with bitterness, "I really think you deserve the same sentence as all the other low down whites in this world."

Mama slapped me across the face, but it was evident the slap had hurt her more than me. She tried to take me in her arms afterwards, but I had simply laughed and walked away.

I closed my eyes tightly to fight back the tears as I thought about how deeply I must have hurt her. "Poor Mama," I softly whispered as I wondered what she was doing at that moment. I could see her sitting in some old chair smiling. I thought about all the times I had wanted to rub that smile off her face, especially when she smiled at white people. No matter what had happened, she had always managed to smile. I shook my head in amazement as I wondered how she had always managed to be so strong. Despite how hard life had been for her, I had never heard her question the Lord. She had such a great love and faith in him that it just didn't seem to matter what trials came her way; it was as if she knew she would make it through. And she had. I felt grateful that Mama had such a binding and loving relationship with the Savior. I had realized since joining the Church that her relationship with him had been, subconsciously, a pillar to me. Though I had not accepted her feelings at the time, she still had given me principles and values that had led me to being worthy to enter the House of the Lord. "Thank you,Mama, for never giving up the fight to teach me, though I know it was a difficult one," I said to myself.

Glancing down at my engagement ring I felt such emptiness and loneliness for John. I wondered if Mama still felt lonely for Daddy. I thought about them and all the happy times I had seen them share. I still missed Daddy deeply. I wondered if he would have been proud of me for what I had done with my life. And I wondered if things would be different; if he would have allowed my brothers to cut me out of the family. I felt certain he would not have. As I thought about Daddy, I smiled as I recalled how he used to snore in his sleep. We all loved to mock his snores and would tell him how he could put any train to shame. My heart ached for him now. Though the time I had left for college was the only time I could recall Daddy ever hugging me, I now longed for his embrace. I thought about the things he had taught me. Never before had I realized how much I had learned from him. He had taught me to have dignity and pride in myself when the world was trying to humiliate me. I thought about all the times Mama lectured us on love. Though Daddy never openly disagreed with her, he would say, generally following one of her lectures,

"Stands up for whose youse is in this here world. If youse don't, nobody else will." Recalling this statement, I thought about all the times he turned the other cheek, many times in front of us. I now realized it was *for* us. Through his own degradation and humiliation he was hoping to make us strong. And he did.

My heart filled with regrets as I thought about all the times I myself had said or done things to hurt him; like the time he had said "youse is." I had laughed at him and told him he did not know correct English. "You're real *dumb,* Daddy," I had said as I continued laughing. He just turned and walked out of the room.

What an uncharitable child I had been. I had failed to consider the fact that Daddy had never had the opportunity to get an education. I fought to control the sobs that were building like a huge wave in my throat. We live and learn in this world; it always seemed too late when I did. I didn't realize I had allowed a loud sob to escape until the man next to me touched my arm and asked if I was okay. I noticed that the people across the aisle were staring at me with concerned looks on their faces. As I looked to the row ahead of them, I found the man in the aisle seat looking over, too. Amidst all the loneliness and hurt, I felt embarrassed. I briefly explained to him that I was missing my family.

As I looked back out the window, I could still feel the touch of the man's hand on my arm. I thought back to a time in high school when we had been playing an all white team in a basketball tournament. As we stood on the side cheering, one of the white players lost control of the ball. Trying to get the ball before it went out of bounds, he accidently ran into me and another cheerleader. We both screamed and started brushing off our arms where he had touched us, as though he had left fleas. The black fans started laughing, and some yelled, "A whitey touched you!" The laughter increased. At first I laughed with them as I acted out my sheer disgust. I thought eventually the laughter and teasing would stop, but every time things got semi-quiet, someone would yell the remark again and bring laughter. By the end of the game, I was practically in tears. At one point I was so angry, I had longed for that white boy to come close enough for me to kick him. I didn't care if they kicked me out of the game.

I looked at my arm where the man had touched it and wondered afterwards why I had even noticed that touch. It was as if I had expected to see fleas there even though I knew now—just as I had known then—that there weren't any. Feeling ashamed for my thoughts, I looked at the man and thanked him for his concern for me. He smiled warmly and told me I was welcome. I then wondered if he was a member of the Church, but I didn't dwell on the speculation long because my thoughts returned to my family, especially Mama.

Not being able to stop thinking about her, I took my journal out of my shoulder bag to write a letter to her—a letter I knew she would never read. Yet, somehow I felt that putting my thoughts of her on paper might bring some comfort to my sad heart.

Dear Mama,

My heart feels a great loneliness for you. At the same time I am filled with a calm, peaceful feeling. I have such a deep gratitude to the Savior for the parents he felt I was worthy to have. How sad it is to realize how the struggles of poverty, inequality, and a fight for self-dignity made me blind to the gems within my home: you and Daddy.

As a child I could never understand why you never prayed for comfort. But now I do. We were your comfort, and our well-being your richness. For now I can so clearly recall how in all your prayers you expressed gratitude for each of us and the happiness we brought to your life. Oh, Mama, We had the greatest jewel right in our midst—a jewel I took for granted, never taking the time to shine or enjoy its warm glow.

Thank you, Mama, for being all you tried to

be and all you were to me. Forgive me for the foolish child I was; accept me for the woman I'm striving to become. I hope I can fill your shoes as a wife and eventually a mother. And Mama, I do want to be a mother someday. I feel so sorry now for all the countless times I tried to hurt you by saying I never wanted to be a mother—especially one like you (though at the time I sincerely meant it). As a child I grew to resent your having babies because the house always seemed so lonely and cold when you were in bed. I was selfish and only thinking about myself. But now I anxiously look forward to the day for a sign of a precious child growing inside me and to know that the Lord has blessed me to "multiply and replenish the earth," as he so blessed you.

I pray I will be able to walk the paths of righteousness with fortitude and love like yours, Mama. Though I know my path will be different from yours, it will also be partly the same. Negative attitudes of people will probably still be great obstacles along the way—people who will still show rejection for me and possibly my children due to the same narrow-mindedness, and imbedded prejudices. But Mama, like you, I will not let trials get me down. Hopefully, I will remember as you always did, that I do not walk alone—that there is always someone beside me to help me make it through any and all obstacles, no matter how great or small.

I paused from my writing as I stared back out the window. I reflected over the many times I had seen Mama display love when someone had been cruel to her. Though I would criticize her for being kind, she never showed any regret for having done what she did. I would then remove my frustrations from her to Johnny.

Johnny! My thoughts quickly drifted to the brother I remember best, though I had not seen him all these years. I now tried to recall how Johnny had become my favorite brother. We were *so* different, such complete opposites. I was skinny; he was tall and stocky. I was always mean, loud, talkative and boastful; he was kindhearted, quiet. Like Daddy, he was a person of few words, but when he spoke, we listened. It seemed he was always quietly coming to my defense, and because of this, I began turning to him when I needed someone to talk to or play with. I couldn't recall Johnny ever raising his voice or showing anger. His comments about whites were few. He would generally just listen to what others had to say, never adding his own feelings.

It seemed he was always doing things for me. He was a giver; I was a taker. He did so much for me that it was obvious I was his favorite. Yet what did I do for him? I think the only time he finally knew how much he meant to me, was when one of his feet had been severely burned from a heavy piece of hot copper. Though the burn had been extremely deep and nasty, the only treatment available was what Mama could provide at home. For some time Daddy felt certain Johnny would lose his foot. Now I know it was Mama's prayers that kept this from happening.

Like the rest of us, Johnny slept in a crowded bed with others. At the time of his burn, Mama made a pad on the floor for him to sleep on. I stayed by Johnny day and night. At first Daddy had told me to go to bed. I did, only to sneak back out once I heard Daddy snoring. Mornings they usually found me sitting looking at Johnny, or asleep on the floor beside him. Mama finally started making a place for me to sleep near him.

I cried a lot as I watched Johnny sweating and moaning in pain. He only moaned when asleep; when awake he never uttered one word of complaint. I felt so helpless. To feel useful I asked Mama to let me wash and change the wrapping around his foot. Mama generally did this daily to keep infection from setting in. The first time I went to do it, I fainted. I had never seen anything so horrible. I had not even realized how swollen Johnny's foot was; I assumed it was huge because of the wrapping. The next time it needed to be changed I made myself do it. I think Johnny felt proud of me. I did.

I was also frightened during this time, scared something awful was going to happen. I was afraid Johnny would leave us. When he slept too long, I constantly asked Mama to come and make sure he was all right. If Mama couldn't come, I would make a loud noise to waken him, and then apologize for it. At night I mostly stayed awake watching him. If he didn't move for a period of time, I would gently push him until he stirred. I had to be reassured he was still with me.

I was truly happy when he finally started to improve: when he stopped being soaked with seat and moaning in pain, when he stopped screaming in his sleep as if reliving the accident, when he asked to sit up and eventually, stand up.

The bond of love between us was definitely unbreakable. At least I thought it was. My eyes filled with tears as I thought about how the relationship ended when I joined the Mormon Church. I closed my eyes tight and rested my head against my seat. I then mentally read the letter I had written him a million times in my mind.

> Johnny, where are you now? Have you suffered my grief? Have you cried with and for me? Did you ever think we would be like this? I must say I never did. I have been hurt and surprised by your lack of response to all that has happened. It's just not like you to say and do nothing. It was always you who would refuse to do things with the rest of your brothers unless I could be included. It was you who stood up in my defense against the rest (and you were much younger and smaller than they). It was you who wanted to die when you thought I would die from pneumonia. You did not want me to die, afraid I would feel alone.
>
> What happened, Johnny? Don't you know I *have been alone* through this turmoil you and my very own family have put me through? Where

> were you? Why have you been silent through the whole ordeal? You were always there when I needed you before—why not this time? I will never accept nor believe that you no longer love me. NEVER! There was once a song I memorized, for it made me think of you, of us, and when we were growing up together. Some of the words were: "My little one, you gave me love and helped me find the sun; and every time that I was down, you would always come around, get my feet back on the ground." I need you, Johnny. I do need to hear you say you still care.

Hearing the announcement that we were starting our descent into the Salt Lake airport, I closed my journal with the unfinished letter to Mama. Ceasing my thoughts of Johnny, I wiped frantically at my flow of tears. "Since you've been a Mormon, seems like all you do is cry," I said to myself in an effort to smile and stop my tears.

As I got off the plane I knew the Strongs would be waiting for me inside the terminal, and for this I was grateful. I longed to feel their arms of love around me. As I neared the door, I recalled how Louise had said that there was a time and a season for all things—"even for families to get back together." I was going to hang on to that thought and the hope that it would come true for me some day.

6
The Ways of God

I lived in the apartment John and I found before leaving for Chicago. The days seemed to have a million hours in them as they slowly crept away. Hardly a single one passed without my thinking about the trip to Chicago. I kept remembering how I had dreaded going—how I had hoped it would soon be over. Now I longed to relive it. I still found it hard to believe I had actually seen some of my brothers—had seen and held Mama close. Each time I thought about her wearing the dress I had sent her over six years ago, I would recall her wearing it at Daddy's funeral and how proud it made me feel. It was as if then and now she still wore it as an expression of love for me.

Thanks to Mom Strong I was able to get some things accomplished for my wedding. The day she and I went to look for my wedding dress was special. We had to look in only one store to find exactly what I wanted. As I stood trying the gown on, I thought about the time Mama had made a white dress for me for graduation. She had washed and rewashed a flour sack to get it soft enough to sew. Somehow she had saved some inexpensive lace for trim. She had cut some buttons off one of her old dresses to place down the front. It was plain, yet simply beautiful. I had had no idea Mama was making it. For days I had been angry and depressed over the fact that I would not have anything decent to wear to graduation. I now recalled how proud Mama had looked when she saw how happy the dress made me: we both had cried—one of the few close moments I had ever allowed Mama to share in my life. She had been so proud of me for having achieved such a milestone in my life: her first child of twenty-four children to graduate from high school.

I now longed for Mama to share this moment with me, and as I stood with the wedding gown on, tears rolling down my cheeks, I turned to show Mom Strong how it looked. She sat staring at me, her own tears clearly visible. She must have sensed a special need, for she quickly rushed over and held me. Many times in my life I have witnessed the Lord answering my need without my asking, and at that moment I so very distinctively felt Mama's arms around me as she quietly whispered, "Youse look beautiful, child." I also felt, for a brief moment, the presence of someone else embracing both of us with the strength, yet gentleness, of Daddy.

Upon arriving home that day, I went and looked at the old "cry-rag" Mama had tucked in my hand the day we left Chicago.I took it and pinned it securely to my wedding gown so it would be near me on my wedding day. I thought about Mama and the Savior. Then I thought about my cousin who had died of Sickle Cell Anemia and of how distraught and angry I had been at God. I thought about how much she wanted to live, to have good health, and yet she never blamed the Lord for her suffering. She always made sure those who did blame him knew that she was aware of his love for her. I recalled how she had kept a sign above her bed during those times that said, "Jesus loves me; this I know, for the Bible tells me so." I thought about how good the Lord had been to me. How he had always been beside me through good and bad times—how he was constantly reaching out and giving me comfort, even when I failed to ask for it. I reflected over the time I had finally allowed my heart to admit that I knew the gospel was true. I had feared the truth, and that night as I lay in bed trying to calm that fear, I kept hearing the words Dr. Martin King, Jr., had said the evening before his death: "Like anybody, I would like to live a long time. Longevity has its place. But I'm not concerned about that now. *I just want to do God's will.*"

As I thought about that night, I knew I should kneel down and thank the Lord for the friend he truly was and always had been to me. I wanted to remind him (though I knew I didn't have to) that I still wanted to do his will, still wanted to dedicate my life in service to him. I wanted him to know that I was sorry for all the times I had spent moping about what I didn't have instead of being happy for the things he had blessed me with. I realized how abundantly the Lord had blessed me with people who loved me and supported me. I knew I would someday have my family again. I had to keep believing and have the patience I had had for the priesthood to be given to my race. I again reflected back to the night I had faced the truthfulness of the gospel and how I had been unable to sleep. I had finally climbed out of bed and sat near a window gazing up at the heavens. As I did, I thought back over my life and all the bitterness I had felt, and how now I felt so fragile—so open to pain. I was afraid of what was going to happen to me. The feeling of love was so new and different. I feared how easily man would be able to hurt me. I felt defenseless. In the wee hours of morning I crawled back into bed, and as I did, I clearly recalled the last words Dr. King had spoken: "I'm happy tonight. I'm not worried about anything. I'm not fearing any man. *Mine eyes have seen the glory of the coming of the Lord.*"

It was late evening when I finally finished reflecting over my life and knelt in prayer to the Lord. I realized how little I had given to him since my engagement to John, how I had canceled so many opportunities to share my testimony even though I might have worked them into my schedule. I recommitted myself to the Lord. I knew that the adversary had tried to destroy me and my testimony through the loss of my family. I knew he could threaten my testimony again. It seemed he had the greatest advantage of succeeding by using those I loved the most. I knew the importance of staying close to the Lord and keeping him first and foremost in my life as I entered this phase of my life.

Somehow I made it through the three months of separation from John, and before long our wedding date was only a night away. I had given him the choice of selecting our temple. He had chosen Oakland.

The night before our wedding was a restless one for all of us. I found it impossible to sleep, and when I went downstairs at

John's home, I found he had apparently been unable to sleep also. His journal lay open on the table. Curiosity compelled me to pick it up and read it, though I knew it was wrong to do so without his permission.

> "I have tried going to bed and sleeping but it's impossible. How can a man sleep when he's getting married tomorrow? It's already after three in the morning and we have to be up at seven. Help, Mr. Wizzard, I don't think I'm going to make it through this night.
>
> All day I have thought of nothing but Mary. There is no one I know who compares to her—no one even comes close. My heart tells me we are right for each other; my spirit tells me we are. This has not waved from day to day. It is not ever a question I wonder about. I will love her to the end and beyond.
>
> Today I thought about the first time I saw her—she was speaking at a fireside in our stake. She was so mysterious—so far away—had so much and was so beautiful. Who was she? How did we get to where we are? The stake was certainly impressed with her talk. I rushed up afterward (leaving my date) to tell her how much I had enjoyed her talk. I really wanted to talk to her, especially ask her for a game of racquetball, but I surmised that people were always trying to get personal with her. MARY STURLAUGSON—what an honor just to be engaged to her. I'm engaged!
>
> I must admit that during the first couple of weeks of our relationship I liked her a lot but I sort of hoped—not hoped, but thought, that at least if she started not to like me then I would not be faced with the difficult decision of marriage and especially marriage to someone black. How

strange, though, that a couple of days later I had a strong desire for her feelings to continue. I'm so thankful that everything worked out for us to be together for eternity. She is the best bride anybody could ever want.

I recall that what impressed me most about our first date was that she was interested in me. She wanted to know what I thought. We both wanted to know about the other's feelings. It was such a refreshing change from all the other girls I had been associated with. It felt great. I wrote the feeling down in my journal that night and also a letter to my mom about it. We had a *good* talk that night, and I wanted it to continue. Our relationship then and now is a good one—it truly is. Together we have a lot of potential which I think we will be able to bring out in each other. She's great, and my respect for her is immense. I love her!

I can still remember the time I went to see her and the fact that she was black wasn't the first thing I thought about. I was so happy just to see—the person. How foolish that I ever allowed her color to be a factor, even for a small moment. It's the person inside that is more important. Profound I know, but what I'm trying to say is that it was when I let go of color that I really began to face my feelings for her. I knew I liked her a lot. Of course I would say I "loved her," but we were reluctant to use that word. I remember sending her flowers later that day and though I am not a poet, I gave it a try. How did it go?

Dear Mary
Roses are dead?
Oh, I think not.
Here is some proof

And I like you a lot.
Furthermore,
Roses aren't black
And that I regret,
But until they progress
Here's the best color yet.

She cried!! I'm not sure if it was because I had not been able to send black roses or if she was touched by my lack of poetic ability. She's great. She's sensitive, too. One Saturday I had to be at school all day to work on a project for a class. She sent me a "care lunch." I thought it ironic—the timing. The package had arrived when Boyd K. Packer was delivering his talk on marriage and its great importance. I was thinking about her, wondering how it might be, imagining how good it could be, just wondering what I could do to be worthy of her. I liked her then—an awful lot.

There are times I don't want to remember—like the time I went with her when she spoke in Levan. I was so nervous going to sit up on the stand with her. I felt that all eyes were on us—as they probably were. It's strange remembering how nervous I was with her in front of others—partially because of her reputation and standing in the Church, but mostly because of her color. Or the time when we were at the Pecks in Idaho and I was still somewhat reluctant to hold hands in front of others. I feel sorry for that now. Sorry that it didn't seem more natural. It was new to me and I really felt self-conscious. Yet it didn't take long for that feeling to melt away. It's strange to think back on it, because it's absolutely nothing to me now. I love her so much. I can't wait to begin our eternal life together. She's such a special child of God, and I think this is such a blessing. I just keep thanking Heavenly Father over and over.

I think I'll stop and see if she's gone to bed. If she hasn't, I am going to ask her to please do so, though. I don't know why. She's probably like me—too excited to sleep. Oh well, I'd better check and see; one of us has got to be awake tomorrow!

She wasn't asleep yet, but said she would try now. My little bride-to-be! I hold such special memories of her, of us. Like the time she told an audience in Tooele how fast I had driven to get her there from another fireside in Bountiful—35 minutes. Everyone was shocked and throughout the packed chapel people whispered "Oh My!" Or I remember the time she came to Rochester, New York, to speak while I was still there on an internship. I had picked her up at the airport, and though it was late at night. I decided to show her some of the city. I got lost and ended up going the wrong way on a one-way street. When the police pulled me over and began questioning me as to why I was going the wrong way *and* why I was in that part of town, he glanced inside and saw Mary. Then he ordered me out of the car and wanted to see my driver's license. As he continued questioning me, I soon realized the street we were on was a disreputable one I had heard about. Feeling totally embarrassed at what the officer must have been thinking, I blundered through my answer. Mary, trying to help, leaned over and said, "Officer, he just picked me up." Mary tells things in such innocence—without thinking. She meant I had just picked her up at the airport, but it sounded like just what the officer expected to hear in this part of town.

Again I remembered the time she met my

mom and how nervous she was. I remember pulling off the freeway before arriving home and trying to ease her fears. I felt so proud the way Mom put her arms around her and gave her reassurance. My parents are *so* special and I love them *a lot!*

Today I was trying to think back on how my attitude toward blacks had been formed. My dad had never allowed any racial comments, I know. Over the years I had many positive feelings and experiences I could list:

• My dad did not allow any racial comments.

• Wanting all through junior high and high school to have a black friend—I'm not sure of the motive or even if there was one.

• A definite empathy for persecuted blacks in movies, like *To Kill A Mocking Bird.*

• Loving it when Mom imported a black man from San Francisco to speak in our ward on the priesthood.

• Making friends with a black man while on my mission in Rhode Island.

• Really sincere disgust when a friend of my dad told a joke about blacks in bad taste. (I was very young.)

• Constantly expressing to my mom and others that blacks were "my favorite minority."

• Honestly and sincerely desiring to adopt black children, an idea which most people—especially the girls I dated—thought was crazy. This has been a desire of mine for quite a number of years—odd but true.

• Getting in a big argument with a companion who used the word N — — — — —

and doing my utmost to defend the cause.

- Wanting to go down to Black Panthers headquarters in Oakland and sign up.
- Desiring to travel in the South. Could it be the feeling came because that's where Mary was at the time? Strange!

There are other things I can't think of now, but they are attitudes I've always had. I cannot believe I have not been prepared for my beautiful bride, even though I never considered marrying someone black. I don't think I even thought such a possibility existed, especially for a temple marriage. I am happy and grateful to be marrying Mary. I think first of her as a person. Then I think of our relationship, then last of all it comes to me—"she's black!" It's like an added extra bonus. I just can't get over it. I don't even feel worthy of such a great blessing.

During the past few years I kept wondering what the problem was—why I couldn't find someone I could really love? I could not figure it out, yet I knew deep down that somehow the Lord had someone for me. I just never dreamed it would be someone so extremely special. Also, during the past few years I had resigned myself to the fact that I would never find anyone as special as my high school sweetheart—a sad thought, really, but Mary had surpassed that. The Lord has actually given me someone more special, someone I love even more. She's beautiful, kind, considerate, loyal, extremely faithful, strong, shy, spiritually great, a good listener, a great sense of humor and she puts up with me!

I'd better go make sure Mary's in bed; it's already 5:48.

I guess she fell asleep with the light on,

> because she didn't answer when I tapped on her door. I want her to be alert and bright tomorrow. I hope she slows down after we are married. She goes and goes, never taking time for herself. I am concerned about her, especially her health. I have watched her go for days eating barely a bit of food—a conditioning from her childhood. I hope I can make sure she takes better care of herself.
>
> I guess I'd best get to bed, too, though I'm not the least bit sleepy. Mary, if you can be patient as I grow, know that I am eager to make you comfortable—I love and trust you. I have confidence in you/us. Know that I do fully expect us to be husband and wife. Just know that I know you are special. I can't wait for us to start our eternal journey together. You make me feel special. I want to live up to whatever Heavenly Father has for me: for us. My preparation relative to your race and our meeting like we did—so unlikely—teaches me much about the ways of God. I love you, honey. Thanks for waiting all these years for me.

I climbed the stairs slowly after reading the things he had written: my eyes filled with tears; my heart swelled with love, joy, and thankfulness for the great young man Heavenly Father had blessed me with for an eternal mate. I hoped and prayed I would be worthy of his love and that we could truly live up to and do all that the Lord might ever want or require of us. As I thought about John's request to be patient as he grows, I thought about how I still had to work at keeping my testimony strong. I recited a couple of scriptures in Alma 32.

> If ye will nourish the word, yea, nourish the tree as it beginneth to grow by your faith with great diligence, and with patience, looking forward to the fruit thereof, it shall take root; and

behold it shall be a tree springing up unto everlasting life . . . Then ye shall reap the rewards of your faith, and diligence, and patience, and long-suffering. . . .

7
My Cup Runneth Over

"You are such a lovely bride," John's mom said. I thanked her as I wondered if she ever thought her son's bride someday would turn out to be black. I felt certain she had not. I loved and admired her dearly for the way she had accepted me, though I'm sure she had experienced some struggles in doing so. I thought about how, two weeks before John and I met, a lady in her ward had asked her if she had read *A Soul So Rebellious.* When John's mom said "no," the woman felt impressed to tell her that she should read it to learn about "this girl's life." I have wondered, since hearing about this incident, if the Lord wasn't preparing her for her son's eternal mate.

"Funny how life sometimes works out," I thought as I sat on a stool in front of the mirrors in the brides' room of the Oakland Temple. As I looked at myself in all white, preparing to be sealed for time and all eternity, it all seemed too good to be true. Me, the skinny runt of the family; the kid who didn't think she would live through the many rough times of childhood. It seemed impossible that I had come so far. I sat, feeling so much gratitude to the Lord who had, in his own gentle way, brought a once proud, rebellious, and reluctant *me* so far. "Why me?" I thought to myself. Of the twenty-four of us, I could not understand why the Savior had chosen me. None of my sisters had been rebellious. Louise probably would have been much easier to work with than I had been. I had been as stubborn and rebellious as my brothers, so it would have made sense for the Lord not to chose any of us to hear his gospel. I silently gave him thanks. I prayed I would not fail him nor whatever work I might be called to do for him.

Staring at my gown in the mirror. I tried to recall seeing a marriage ceremony in my family. The only wedding I could remember was for Louise, the others before her had gone to a justice of the peace. A feeling of sadness went through me as I thought about Louise's wedding.

Daddy could not even afford a small church wedding for her. She was married in our old living room in the presence of only the minister and his wife, and all of us children who stood watching intently, with dirty faces and dirty clothes. Louise had worn one of Mama's dresses; not that Mama's dress was new, or even close to being so. In fact, it had enough patches on it to represent each of her children, plus a dozen or more neighborhood kids. Louise had worn it because of the length; it hung almost to her ankles and gave her the feeling that she was wearing a long gown.

None of this seemed to matter to Louise. She radiated happiness. After she had taken her vows and the ceremony ended, she turned toward Mama and Daddy and told them how much she loved them. She thanked them for all they had done for her, then quickly glanced at each of us and told us she would miss us and that we (she looked directly at me) should "be good" to Mama and Daddy.

We had never been close, yet I cried as I watched her and her husband drive away to begin their new life together in Chicago. Later when I had gone into the room we shared with the others, though I thought about the extra space we would now have in the old bed, I still felt sad that she was gone.

I again looked at myself in the mirror at the beautiful, flowing white gown I was wearing. A feeling of guilt went through me. Louise was the one who truly deserved to be having such a day, not me. I felt so richly blessed, and I again asked the Lord: "Why me?" What had I ever done that he should be so good to me? I wanted so much at that moment to turn back the hands of time and somehow share all I had with Louise, especially the gospel. For it was indeed the gospel that had brought me this far. Recalling how things had gone between

Louise and me in Chicago, I longed to have her there with me, to be able to again tell her I loved her.

"Would you come with me?"

I turned to see a lovely little old temple worker standing directly behind me. I had not seen her walk up, though I had been looking in the mirror. As I stood up, she took both my hands in hers.

"My, you are a beautiful bride!" she said warmly. She stepped back and admired me for a moment. "I remember many, many years ago when I was getting married," she continued, smiling sweetly as if deep in thought. "Everything had gone wrong that morning—even the sky was black and dreary. But, even though the day began with a very dismal morning, when I looked at myself dressed in white and standing in the holy house of the Lord, I felt only tranquility and happiness. Enjoy this event, *every* second of it. This is the only moment like this you will ever have. Enjoy it!" she said emphatically. "You are beautiful. Your young man must be so proud to know that you are going to be his for eternity."

As we left the bride's room she asked if my family were there, I told her no, but my husband's family was. She asked how long had they been members of the Church. When I answered,"all their life," she stopped and looked at me proudly. "How special to be marrying into such a family; to think your young man stayed with the Church all his life *even* during the time he could not hold the priesthood," she said, ending her words on a sympathetic note. "But he has always held the priesthood," I said as we resumed our walk. She stopped suddenly. "Either your young man is awfully young—like about . . ." She stopped and looked as though she were adding something up in her head. ". . . like about three years old or you have some wrong information. But let's not ruin your day. That's irrelevant now. The important thing is that you two are able to have the blessing of a temple marriage."

When we arrived in the Celestial Room, she looked around as if searching for someone. "Well, I guess your young man hasn't finished dressing yet." Just as she finished her words,

John walked up to me and said, "Hi, honey," and took hold of my hand. I heard the temple worker gasp. When I saw the look on her face, I realized she had not been expecting to see John, and then it dawned on me why. I hadn't thought to tell her that "my young man" was not black.

"I see why you said what you said." The woman now hesitated, sounding flustered. She then wished us well and left.

I didn't dwell on the incident. Instead, I looked with pride at my "young man." He was so handsome. All my thoughts centered on him—thoughts filled with joy. *How I wished my daddy had lived long enough to meet you,* I thought as I looked at him. My heart ached for Mama and Daddy to see him—to see us—at this choice moment in our lives.

"You look gorgeous," John said, stepping back to look at me. He raved about my wedding dress and I felt proud that I had chosen a design pleasing to his taste (and mine). "So, this is my beautiful bride, and she's black," he said with enthusiasm. I started crying! John looked puzzled. "Did I say somethig wrong, honey?" he asked with a sad look in his eyes. I shook my head as I tried explaining my desire to have Mama there and to have had Daddy live long enough to be with us, too. John tried to console me, telling me the Lord would, somehow, enable them to experience this day with me. At that moment, a temple worker walked over and asked us to follow her.

I had sent out invitations to our sealing, requesting that everyone who attended would wear white. When we walked into the sealing room filled with people dressed in white, John looked at me and whispered, "Well, you got your all-white sealing."

The spirit in the sealing room was overpowering. Looking slowly around at the people, I saw radiating smiles. Most of the women had tears in their eyes. Tears filled my eyes when I saw how many had traveled great distances to share in this occasion. The Allies, my first foster family—my first sounding board when I moved to Utah—had flown out to be with us. I saw President and Sister Bishop, the mission president at the time I was baptized. Looking at President Bishop, I wondered if he had ever considered the important role he had played as an instrument in the hands of the Lord as he had encouraged the missionaries not to give up on me. Despite her health, Grandma Reeder had traveled the great distance to be with me. The Mortensens were there, even though I knew Brother Mortensen detested nothing more than driving in California. So many came from far and near. What had I done to be worthy of their love and support? Nothing, yet they had come.

I slowly continued to look at the many people gathered there. Then my eyes froze. Seated among all the people was a man I had seen briefly several times before but never fully understood why he continued to appear in my life. As I stared at him, my mind quickly flashed back to those times I had seen him.

The first time had been on a morning I was on my way to class at BYU shortly after moving to Utah. On this particular morning I had just finished a brief conversation with two girls. Still smiling from our conversation, I turned to continue on to class. As I did, I came face to face with a young man who looked straight into my eyes, but said nothing. He then stepped aside and continued on his way. I stared at him as he walked away, feeling certain I knew him, and wondering if he felt he knew me. I was somewhat disturbed as to why he hadn't said "hello" or "pardon me." The next day, at a completely different time, we again passed each other. This time he again looked at me, but said nothing. This same event continued for the rest of that week and into the next. It didn't seem to matter what hour of the day I took that path, we always met. Midway through the second week I started to feel paranoid as I kept feeling I knew him from somewhere. Yet, I had made the decision that I was not going to be the one to speak first!

One Saturday as I was about to leave the apartment for my self-defense class, I paused at the door and said another prayer. I pleaded with the Lord "not to let me see that same person." As I proceeded to class I felt good. In fact, I was humming and kicking a rock here and there. Then it happened. I looked up from kicking the rock, and ahead of me was that same young man. Though he was ahead of me and going in the same direction, I knew he was the same one. I slowed my pace to make sure I didn't catch him, and then I quickly bowed my head and asked the Lord why he had allowed my day to be ruined. When I opened my eyes—though they had been closed for only a brief moment—I was only a hand's length behind him. I nearly died of shock. I finally decided to quicken my pace and pass him. I had decided I definitely was not going to look at him. But just when I got directly across from him, my head turned in his direction and my eyes stared into warm, loving eyes. I heard myself say "Morning" as I rushed past. When I got a few paces ahead of him I heard him say, "Good morning, Mary." I didn't slow my pace down until it dawned on me that he had spoken my name. I came to an abrupt halt as I thought, "Why that creep even knows my name." I turned to confront him about the past several days. He was nowhere to be seen. At first I thought "how strange," but because there were many different paths I assumed he had taken one in a different direction.

I never saw him again on that path. At Christmastime of the following year I tried to see my family, but they turned me away at the door. I had finally gone over to one of Daddy's sisters to stay overnight before returning to Utah. As I drove up to my aunt's house, a group of children were following what looked to be a bum—a white one at that. Yelling nasty comments, one after the other would run up and try to kick him. The bum just continued as though he were not aware of the kids at all, nor what they were doing to him. Once I got inside, I asked my aunt who he was. She just nonchalantly said some bum that had shown up a few days ago that generally went past her place each day about this time. It was early evening. She also said she was surprised he hadn't been hurt or killed wandering on our side of town. That night had been a restless one for me. I could not sleep, knowing that although my family lived only a few miles away, I couldn't see them, couldn't be with them. I cried almost all of that night. By morning I finally decided that I would give up the gospel for them. I begged the Lord to understand, and thanked him for having done all he did for me. I told him I still knew the gospel was true—that fact would never change for me—but now I needed my family. Around noon I was prepared to let my brothers know of my decision. My aunt had fixed some sandwiches, and we were about to sit down to eat when I heard loud noises from the children outside. Looking out the window, I could see the bum coming up the street. I don't know why, but something inside me prompted me to grab a few of the sandwiches on a plate. I then made a quick dash for the door.

My aunt's daughter must have sensed I was going to give them to the bum, because as I started for the door, she yelled, "Girl, don't you feed that white trash on my mama's good plate."

I made another mad dash for the kitchen as she handed me a paper one and said, "It's true. You do love those white people, don't you?" She shook her head in disbelief. I swallowed hard, knowing that though they were aware of what had taken place in my life, they lacked understanding. I quickly switched plates and left.

As I made it outside with the sandwiches, the bum had already gone past the house and a few blocks down the street. I yelled "mister!" once, a second time, and a third time before I was directly behind him. He turned to look at me and I froze, staring at him in complete bewilderment. Though the face looked old and wrinkled beneath the straggly gray beard, I knew those eyes. As I continued staring into his eyes, I slowly handed him the plate. When he took it, he said "Bless you, Mary," then turned and continued on his way. The little children had stopped their teasing to watch me. I stood watching him until he turned up another street and out of sight.

After that, I didn't go to see my family, for I knew I could not and would not sacrifice the gospel to be accepted by them or by anyone.

I did not see those eyes again until the day of the priesthood revelation. I had rushed over to the campus to find Brother Clark V. Johnson to share the excitement of the news with him. As I was about to knock on his office door, I was startled when a male voice said, "A glorious day, Mary." I turned and was about to say, "One of the greatest," but my words froze inside as our eyes met for a brief moment. I stared at him in silence as he rounded the corner and out of view.

When I went through the temple for my endowments in preparation to go on a mission, I again saw him. He had stood by one of the doors observing, as I embraced the people gathered in the Celestial room.

And now today—my wedding day. I stared at him. He had never frightened me. Amidst my surprise and shock, I had always felt from him a warm, loving feeling. Tears built and slowly rolled down my face as I recalled the day of my baptism and realized why he had seemed familiar that day on my way to class. He had been present at my baptism, too. Mom Strong, seated next to me, began to offer a handkerchief as my sobs became noticeable, but I shook my head "No." Easing my hand inside the edge of my sleeve, I removed the old rag (unwashed and still in a crinkled ball) that Mama had given me that day in Chicago. I carried it with me today as a tribute of love for Mama.

As John and I went to the altar to make our covenants to each other before the Lord, I again looked at the strange man. Our eyes met, and we smiled. As I knelt before the altar, I knew that when my covenants were completed, he would no longer be there. Upon completing them—hoping I would be wrong—I immediately turned to look. He was gone. As on the day of my baptism, I felt sad, disappointed, and yet deeply grateful that he had shared another important event in my life.

Feeling grateful again for all that I had, especially the true gospel of Jesus Christ, I turned and thanked our sealer, President Nicolaysen. John and I then held each other close with gratitude for each other and for the step we had just taken together. The rest of the people came over to congratulate us.

Happy sobs filled my throat when Elder Sekona, the missionary who had persevered in his efforts to share the true gospel—who had not given up, but accomplished what the Lord had asked of him—walked up. Without saying a word we embraced with jubilation as we both cried with happiness.

"Thank you for not giving up on me," I said repeatedly. "You made this moment possible."

John was watching us with a look of concern. I introduced

him to Elder Sekona. Recognizing the name, he, too, embraced Elder Sekona. "Thank you for finding my wife and sharing the gospel with her," he said, his voice breaking, and tears falling. "You have made this day possible for us," he emphasized with joy.

"That was my line," I said to John as the three of us embraced, laughing, and the tears pouring down our faces. At that moment, President Bishop walked over to us and asked if he might share in this great moment, as he encircled as many of the three of us as he could.

President Bishop and Elder Sekona had barely left when John's grandmother walked up to us. Seeing her, I thought how our dating and eventual engagement had affected her. She had always dreamed of someday having blond-haired, blue-eyed grandchildren. Our relationship had brought her much grief. As I sensed the despair and pain she had suffered, sadness and sorrow filled my heart. I felt I understood somewhat how deeply this had affected her. John and his sister Dani were the only children who would continue her posterity. As I looked at her hugging John, I wanted to express the emotions that were stirring inside me, to somehow seek her forgiveness for bringing heartache and disappointment to her. Soon she stood in front of me, head down, as if trying to formulate something to say. With a hopeless gesture, she pulled me into her arms, and I closed mine around her as we had a good cry together. "I'm sorry for the way I treated you," she said with sincere emotion. Breaking the embrace with one of her arms, she drew John closer to us and told us she was truly happy for us and would support us all she could. Wishing us well, she left.

I did not think my heart could handle much more excitement. I already felt as though it were going to burst. But I was wrong; there was still more to come.

It was not until I tried to wipe away the steady flow of tears did I see—or discover—what I had in my hand. Trying to find a dry spot on Mama's old rag, I opened it up for the first time since I had it. Something fell to the floor. Embarrassed, I quickly, though gracefully and discreetly, picked it up. Seeing that it was only an old worn piece of paper, I tried to think of what to do with it. Finally, I decided to tuck it up my sleeve. The thought then occurred to me that maybe Mama had left a message there. Trying to control my excitement, I pulled the paper out. I didn't worry about making noise—the crispness of the paper had long been worn away.

As I tried to smooth out the wrinkles, I was able to see that something was written on it. I wondered how many years Mama had kept this note. The letters were almost faded beyond recognition. My heart seemed to stop when I saw what it said: "SLY" (someone loves you). I gasped as I said "Johnny," placing my hand over my mouth in disbelief and happiness. "What, honey?" John asked leaning closer.

I had not meant to say it aloud, but I had. "This is more than I ever thought could happen to me in one day," I said.

He hugged me close, apparently thinking I was referring to him and the sealing.

"Thank you, Lord, for all that has happened this day, for my cup surely runneth over," I silently prayed.

8
Yea, Though I Walk. . .

"Push, honey," John was saying. I was on the delivery table for the final stage of my pregnancy.

"Hey, what about an epidural?" I said.

"Are you in much pain?" the nurse asked.

"No," I replied. "I'm not in any pain, but according to all I have read and heard, I should have an epidural."

"It's too late to give you one now," the nurse said. "Your baby is already on the way."

"So what do I do?" I asked her, feeling afraid, though it seemed there wasn't yet enough pain to warrant medication.

"Push," she said. "Push."

I looked at John, and he nodded his head encouragingly. "But I'm tired," I said, wanting desperately to sleep.

"Soon, honey," John said. "The baby is almost here, and you have done just great so far. The baby needs you to push in order to complete his or her journey into this life." He looked so excited.

Tears filled my eyes as I reflected over the time we had been told that I probably would not be able to have any children. Not only had our first Christmas together as husband and wife been ruined by my illness but the sharp pains that had unceasingly ripped through the lower part of my stomach had forced us home early from our Christmas vacation in hopes of finding out the problem. We had sat in Dr. Bigler's office in a daze, unable to believe what we had just heard.

"There's only a fifty-fifty chance you'll have a full-term birth," he said, "and those chances decrease with time."

He and John talked more, but I had sat speechless, feeling numb. All I had wanted was to get home, to close the world out. I needed time: time to pray, time to think, time to hope, time to cry.

I had not shared with John the feelings of turmoil steadily building inside me. Instead, we had driven home in silence that cold January day less than six months after we were married. I kept thinking: love, marriage, life—the three should have brought elation to me. But now I felt only depression. Tears had been close to falling, yet they stayed as if waiting for the right cue. Bitterness toward the Lord had wanted to seep in, but my love for him was too great. I had felt the need to pray, but words wouldn't formulate into sentences. Questions and more questions had pounded at my mind, but I had refused to concentrate on any particular one for fear the dam that had built up inside would break, and with the break would come uncontrollable emotions. My head hurt; the pain had become most excruciating. I recall wanting all the questions pounding inside me to stop, wanting life to withhold so much pains and trials. I wondered why all I wanted in life seemed to be obtained only through periods of suffering. I wanted only for once to be able to enjoy a chapter of my life without the suffering, without the trials, without the worry, without the failures, without the hurting. I wondered how I could show the Lord that he could trust and have faith in me without having to test me. I wanted the blessings I desired most to come without trials.

"Oh, Lord," I had thought, fighting back the tears, "I'm so tired, so tired of fighting, so tired of the struggles of life. Don't you know I love you? Haven't I proven in times past that I would sacrifice and endure all for you? Not again, please. Please let this one pass. Please do not allow me to be robbed of something I so dearly desire."

When we had arrived home, I asked John to allow me to be alone for a little while. I had gone into our bedroom, picked up our wedding album, and sat on the edge of the bed. I stared at the picture of us on our wedding day standing in front of the Oakland temple, smiling happily into each other's eyes, exhilarated with the future of unfulfilled dreams and plans awaiting us. Tears formed heavily in my eyes, slowly rolled down my cheeks and onto the album. I gently wiped them off and replaced the album on the nightstand, then reclined slowly onto the bed. I soon realized what a mistake that had been. Next to my head was the little black doll John's mom had given me shortly after we were married. When I saw the doll and thought of the dreams it represented, the dam broke.

John had tapped on the bedroom door as he slowly opened it. He then stood as if debating whether or not to come in. He looked at me sadly and asked, "Are you okay, honey?"

"Hold me," I had said pleadingly. The words were barely spoken before he had me in his arms. We cried, talked, and cried some more.

"I love you, Mary," he had said in earnestness, "and this love will not change or die if you cannot have children. I brought something I want you to reread and *this time* fully comprehend the word *fight* in its entirety." He pulled out a letter from his shirt pocket that he had written to me while in Rochester and handed it to me to read. As I read it, I thought about the incident that had inspired him to write it. Some girl at church had used the word *nigger*. It hurt John deeply. Looking at her he had said, "Please don't use that word. The girl I am about to spend eternity with happens to be black." Now as I reread his letter my eyes again filled with tears and gratitude for him.

> . . . As I look at your picture, it just makes me cry to think of people saying that word, especially to you.
>
> I look over at Raggedy-Ann (I had given him my black Raggedy-Ann doll to take with him to New York), and it's like seeing someone treat that cute, harmless thing like dirt for something it had no control over—or even if it did, why hurt it? It never did anything. How can people purposefully hurt their fellowmen so? I don't understand this word sometimes.

> I love you, Mary, very much and will fight with you against racism or any other fight you might encounter along the way. I suppose I would have a much easier marriage with a white girl—not the relationship itself, but with the perception of the relationship as viewed by others. But I wouldn't trade you for anyone in the world. I love you and am prepared to accept *any* challenge that comes to us. I hurt with your hurts; I triumph in your victories.

"Your fight—*our* fight—is to keep on believing in the mercy and goodness of the Lord," he had said when I completed reading the letter. "The Lord has been good to you, Mary. He heard and blessed you with the desire of your heart when you wanted to serve a mission; he will hear and bless you again. But we must be willing to accept his blessings however he chooses to grant them to us. If he grants us children—created by us or by some other means: through adoption service, as foster parents, whatever—let's be ready and willing to accept his blessing with all the gratitude we have, for he would have heard and answered our prayers. Your patriarchal blessing says, 'You shall receive children as a sacred trust from your Father in Heaven.' Believe that you will. Never forget it nor my everlasting love for you."

Looking at John now, I felt sorry for all the difficult times we had had. I didn't say it verbally but with my eyes. Yet he heard me. "I love you, too," he said smiling. "Now push so our baby can get here," he added enthusiastically. All in the delivery room laughed. I tried muscling the energy to push. I prayed, though I remembered clearly all of the complications of my pregnancy, that the baby about to be born to us would be healthy.

My Little Friend

Who are you—my little one,
Heaven sent in a body so frail and small?
Yet with a strong and very determined spirit,
Ready and willing to conquer all.

They say people can become close friends,
As they struggle together through trials.
Our friendship was already cemented before,
And after you traveled the birth canal—
Seeming to extend for miles.

You must have a very special mission,
To perform here on earth at this time.
You are our miracle baby—
Whom it was said, this earthly mountain,
Was too hard for you to climb.

Welcome to mortality, my friend.
I pray your little body is healthy.
We've already, together, passed obstacles.
You're priceless—I feel so wealthy.

There's so much Daddy and I have to show you,
To talk about and do.
Please stay with us long enough, little one.
May our love be a strength to see you through.

Jeanette Blanchard

(Used with permission of author)